GCSE ICT *for* CCEA

Siobhan Matthewson
Gerry Lynch

PART OF HACHETTE LIVRE UK

The Publishers would like to thank the following for permission to reproduce copyright material:
Photo credits: p.30 *c* Peter Menzel/Science Photo Library, *b* Thanh Do/iStockphoto.com; p.33 *c* Mike McCune/iStockphoto.com, *b* Corbis; p.37 Roger Pilkington/iStockphoto.com; p.47 *t* Mark Karrass/Corbis; p.60 *b* Raritan; p.63 TEK Image/Science Photo Library; p.79 *l* Corbis, *r* Laurie Knight/iStockphoto.com; p.95 Actinic.
Acknowledgements: p.10 *tl* and *b* Google, *tr* Ask; p. 92 and 93 Easyjet.com.
Every effort has been made to trace all copyright holders, but if any have been inadvertently overlooked the Publishers will be pleased to make the necessary arrangements at the first opportunity.

t = top, *b* = bottom, *l* = left, *r* = right, *c* = centre

Screenshots reprinted by permission of Microsoft Corporation, Microsoft and Windows are trademarks of Microsoft Corporation.

Past examination questions reprinted by kind permission of CCEA.

Orders: please contact Bookpoint Ltd, 130 Milton Park, Abingdon, Oxon OX14 4SB. Telephone: (44) 01235 827720. Fax: (44) 01235 400454. Lines are open 9.00 – 5.00, Monday to Saturday, with a 24-hour message answering service. Visit our website at www.hoddereducation.co.uk

First published in 2008 by Hodder Education
a member of the Hachette Livre UK Group
338 Euston Road
London NW1 3BH

Impression number 5 4 3 2 1
Year 2012 2011 2010 2009 2008

Cover photo Photodisk Collection/Getty Images
Typeset in 9pt CentITC Lt BT by Pantek Arts Ltd
Printed in Malta

A catalogue record for this title is available from the British Library

ISBN-13: 978 0340 946 626

Contents

	Introduction	1
1	Unit C1: Knowledge, understanding and skills in communicating, handling information and modelling	7
2	Unit C2: Understanding of ICT systems in everyday life	27
	C2(a) Knowledge of ICT components	27
	C2(b) Information systems	44
	C2(c) Digital communication systems	58
	C2(d) Appplications of ICT	74
3	Unit C3: Implications of ICT for individuals, organisations and society	96
4	Acronyms and abbreviations	113
	Answers	114
	Index	122

Introduction

The purpose of this revision book is to help you gain the best possible outcome when you take CCEA GCSE ICT Full or Short course.

The book outlines the structure of the course and explains the key facts about ICT contained within the specification. The chapters in this book are arranged in a similar order to its companion text, *Information and Communication Technology for CCEA GCSE*, although some of the individual chapters in that book are combined in this book. In each chapter the most important concepts are explained and key definitions are given. The acronyms associated with each section are expanded and students can test themselves using the questions at the end of each section. There is a large variety of questions offering 1 or 2 marks, which is typical of the examination itself. Some 3 mark questions have been included where appropriate, and a number of 5 mark questions based on unit C3 can be used as practice for a typical paper 2 'social impacts' question. The answers to these questions have been included in Chapter 5. Also at the end of each section is a set of past examination questions (without answers) that may be suitable for homework.

Parts of the book that are only applicable to students taking the Full Course are highlighted in grey so that they can be clearly identified.

How to prepare for the CCEA GCSE ICT examination

Know the structure of your course

Are you a Short Course candidate?

Short Course GCSE ICT	Foundation	Higher
1 Written Paper, questions based on the specification	Short Course Paper (Foundation) – 1 hour 40%	Short Course Paper (Higher) – 1 hour 30 minutes 40%
	Four CCEA set assignments internally assessed and externally moderated 60%	Four CCEA set assignments internally assessed and externally moderated 60%

Are you a Full Course candidate?

Full Course GCSE ICT	Foundation	Higher
2 Written Papers, questions based on the specification	Paper 1 – 1 hour Paper 2 – 1 hour 40% (20% for each paper)	Paper 1 – 1 hour 30 minutes Paper 2 – 1 hour 40% (20% for each paper)
	Six CCEA set assignments internally assessed and externally moderated 60%	Six CCEA set assignments internally assessed and externally moderated 60%

Note to help you structure your revision

Paper 1 Full Course Foundation and Short Course Foundation Papers are identical.
Paper 1 Full Course Higher and Short Course Higher Papers are identical.

A more detailed look at the structure of CCEA GCSE ICT

Both the Short and Full Courses have three units. There is a lot of common content. The lists below show the Full and Short Course content.
Sections highlighted in grey are included ONLY on the Full Course.
If you are studying the Short Course you will not need to learn the sections highlighted in grey. The units are as follows.

Unit C1: Knowledge, understanding and skills in communicating, handling information and modelling

Much of the information needed for this unit will be gained through the completion of your coursework.

Unit C2: Understanding of ICT systems in everyday life

This is the main theory unit and contains the following sections:

- Knowledge of ICT components
  - Typical components of a PC
  - Input devices
  - Output devices
  - Storage devices
- Information systems
  - Information and data
  - Data capture
  - Data checking
  - Data structure
  - Data portability
- Digital communication systems
  - Networks (LAN)
  - Internet (WAN)
  - Network security
  - Communicating on a network.
- Applications
  - Electronic monetary processing
  - Computers in control
  - Online services
  - Billing
  - Virtual reality

Unit C3: Implications of ICT for individuals, organisations and society

- Implications of ICT on
  - Education
  - Employment
  - Home and leisure
- Laws
  - Data Protection Act
  - Copyright Designs and Patents Act
  - Computer Misuse Act
  - Health and safety issues
  - Security and privacy issues

Some helpful hints

Understanding questions

Before moving on to the specification content, it may be helpful to look at ways in which students can improve their responses to questions. An examiner can only mark what is written on the paper, they cannot interpret your answer or give marks for what they think you might mean.
Some questions in ICT examination papers start with a 'command' word as in the table below. These words tell you what to do to answer the question.

Command word	Meaning
Expand	Usually used as 'expand the acronym'. Write down what each letter in the acronym stands for.
Complete	Answer in the blank spaces that have been provided. This is sometimes a table or an answer line.
Give/name/state	Only a short answer is required, no explanation.
Tick	Place a tick(s) beside the correct answer(s) in the list.
Circle	Draw a circle around.
(Explain) Why	Give an explanation of why.
(Explain) How	Give an explanation of how.
(Explain) What	Give an explanation of what.
Apart from	Do not use the example following the words 'Apart from' in your answer.
Which	Select one from a number of options presented.
List	Make a list – usually short answers.
Discuss	Give a detailed account including advantages and disadvantages.

Questions also have a 'stem'. Students often restate the stem of the question in their answers, but no credit is given for this in the examination.
For example:

Question: What is data logging?
Answer: Using the computer to log data.

In this answer the student has restated the stem of the question and will receive no marks.
Some correct answers would be:

Collecting data over a period of time without human intervention.
Measuring values at given intervals and recording the values directly onto a computer.

Consider the following:

Question: What does interactive mean?
Answer: Interactive means that a person has access to games and can watch movies at a convenient time by pressing the red button.

In this answer the student has given examples of interaction but has not explained what interactive means. Therefore they obtain no marks. This is a classic example of misinterpreting the question. The student clearly knows how to interact with digital TV but has not explained what interaction actually is.
A correct answer would be:

- To send and receive information.

Two mark questions

For full marks you must make two points. For example consider the following:

Question: What is a wizard? (worth two marks)
Answer 1: A wizard is a step-by-step guide.
Answer 2: A wizard is a program which guides the user step by step to complete a task.

Answer 1 would get one mark. Answer 2 would get two marks since the student made two points – the first: it is a program; the second: it guides the user step by step.

Three mark questions

Questions worth three marks generally require you to list, name or give three explicit answers. You are rarely required to write a paragraph type answer worth three marks.

Unacceptable answers

It is generally accepted that it can be 'faster' to do something using technology or that some technology means that costs are lessened. Whilst this may be the case, in general no marks are awarded for answers such as 'cheaper' or 'faster' without an explanation. You should always include a reason why something is 'cheaper' or 'faster'. Your answers should start 'Cheaper because…' or 'Faster because….'.

Learn all acronyms

Learn all of the acronyms given in Chapter 4. Many of these will come up in the actual examination.
At Foundation level the question is asked as follows:
What do the letters LAN stand for? Answer: Local Area Network.
At Higher level the same question is asked as follows:
Expand the acronym LAN. Answer: Local Area Network.

Paper 1

The content for Paper 1 can be found in the Short Course specification. Remember it is not just the theory but the practical elements undertaken in your coursework which can be examined.

Paper 2

For full course candidates only
This paper includes all of the topics highlighted in grey in addition to any other topic covered on the Short course.

1

Unit C1: Knowledge, understanding and skills in communicating, handling information and modelling

This chapter will cover the features of a range of software packages that you have used in coursework. The range of software includes:

- Web browser software
- Web creation software
- E-mail/conferencing software
- Word-processing/DTP software
- Presentation software
- Graphics software
- Database software
- Spreadsheet software

The coursework component allows you to demonstrate your skills in using a range of packages but the examinations will also assess your knowledge and understanding in these software packages. You need to:

- suggest a suitable package and give reasons for your choice in a given application
- be able to describe up to three features for each package
- be able to explain how to perform a common activity in a given software package
- expand all relevant acronyms stated in this chapter
- define all relevant ICT terms associated with this chapter.

Acronyms and abbreviations

Acronym/abbreviation	Meaning
HTML	HyperText Mark-up Language
WWW	World Wide Web
Cc	Carbon Copy
Bcc	Blind Carbon Copy
ISP	Internet Service Provider
RTF	Rich Text Format
WYSIWYG	What You See Is What You Get
JPEG	Joint Photographic Experts Group

Definitions required

Term	Definition
Web browser	A software application that enables a user to display and interact with text and graphics on web pages in a website. It allows the user to use hyperlinks to other web pages at the same or different website.
MP3	Digital audio encoding in compressed format which is designed to greatly reduce the amount of data required to represent audio, yet still sound like the original uncompressed audio.
Search engine	A program that searches documents/databases for specified keywords or phrases and returns a list of where the keywords or phrases were found.
Hyperlink	An element (text or graphic) in an electronic document that links to another place in the same document or to an entirely different document. These documents could be web pages on a website.
Word processor	A software package that enables you to create a document, store it electronically, display it on a screen, modify it (usually using a keyboard) and print it on a printer.
Web authoring	A software package that enables the user to develop a website. The software will automatically generate the required HTML code for the layout of the web pages based on what the user designs.
e-mail	Short for electronic mail which is the transmission of messages over communication networks. The messages can be notes entered from the keyboard or electronic files stored on a storage medium. Files that are stored are usually attached to e-mails.
Template	A basic structure for a document and contains a number of document settings such as predefined page layout. The use of templates leads to consistently produced documents.
Wizard	A help utility within an application that helps you use the application to perform a particular task. It will take the user through the task in a number of steps offering a finite number of options. Usually one of the options is defaulted.

Animation	The simulation of movement by presentation of a sequence of slightly different still pictures.
Relational database	A complex database structure that can hold a variety of data items in tables. The data items stored in different tables can be linked together.
Table	Refers to data arranged in rows and columns. A spreadsheet, for example, is a table. In a typical database package, all data is stored in tables.
Primary key	One of the fields in a database is designated as the primary key, and must hold a unique value for each record. This is useful when searching for an occurrence of a record.
Spreadsheet	A table of cells arranged in rows and columns. You can define what type of data is in each cell and how different cells depend on one another. Formulas, text, numbers etc. can be entered into the cells.
Macro	A symbol, name or key that represents a list of commands, actions or keystrokes. Many programs allow you to create macros so that you can enter a single character or word to perform a whole series of actions.

Web browsers and search engines

- Microsoft Internet Explorer and Netscape Navigator are examples of web browsers.
- Web browsers have common features that include:

Feature	Description
Back, Forward	Allow the user to visit the previous or next pages viewed.
Refresh	Allows the user to automatically update the web page to take account of any changes that have occurred since the web page was downloaded.
Home	Allows the user to return to the home page on a website.
Search	Keywords or phrases allow the user to search a website for relevant information.
Favourites/Bookmarks	Allows users to store web pages that they frequently access.
Media	This can be used to search for a certain type of media file such as an MP3 file.
History	This is used to show websites that have been accessed in the last number of days or even weeks. This timescale can be set by the user.
Print	Allows the user to print the current web page(s).
e-mail	Launches your e-mail account.

- Search engines allow users to enter keywords/phrases to find information.
- Each search engine has access to a large database of websites.
- Examples of search engines include Google and Ask Jeeves.
- Search engines also include an advanced search facility for more experienced users.

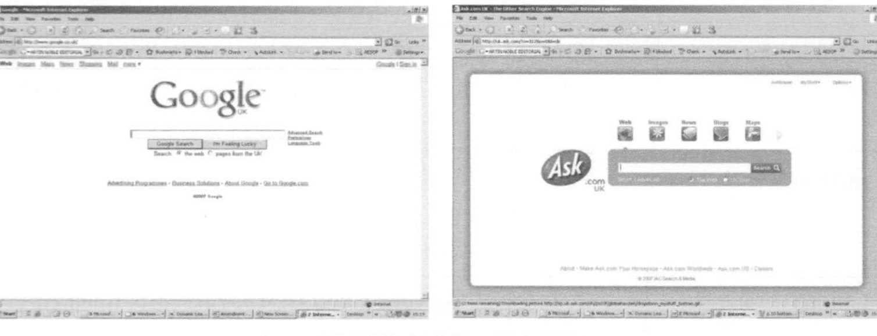

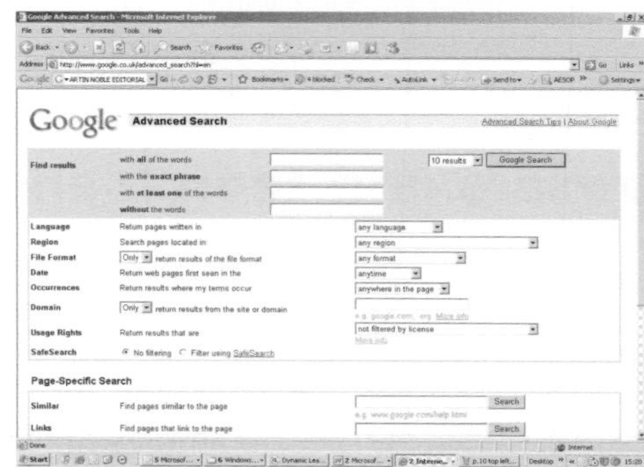

Figure 1.1 Examples of popular search engines

Searching techniques

Technique	Description
Using capital/small letters	Returns websites that consist of both lower and upper case versions of websites.
Using wildcards	The asterisk (*) acts as any character in a keyword. For example, entering Colo*r returns color and colour.
Quotation marks	Using quotation marks (" ") around keywords or phrases will assist in more exact searches.
Keywords first	If you enter the list of words in your phrase in order of importance, it will lead to a better search.
Plus (+) and minus(–)	Using plus and minus (hyphen) signs in front of keywords allows the user to force inclusion (+) or exclusion (–) from phrases.
Complex logic	This involves using AND, OR and NOT school AND pupil [returns websites that contain both "school" and "pupil"] school OR pupil [returns websites that contain either "school" or "pupil"] school NOT pupil [returns websites that contain "school" but not "pupil"]

Web design software

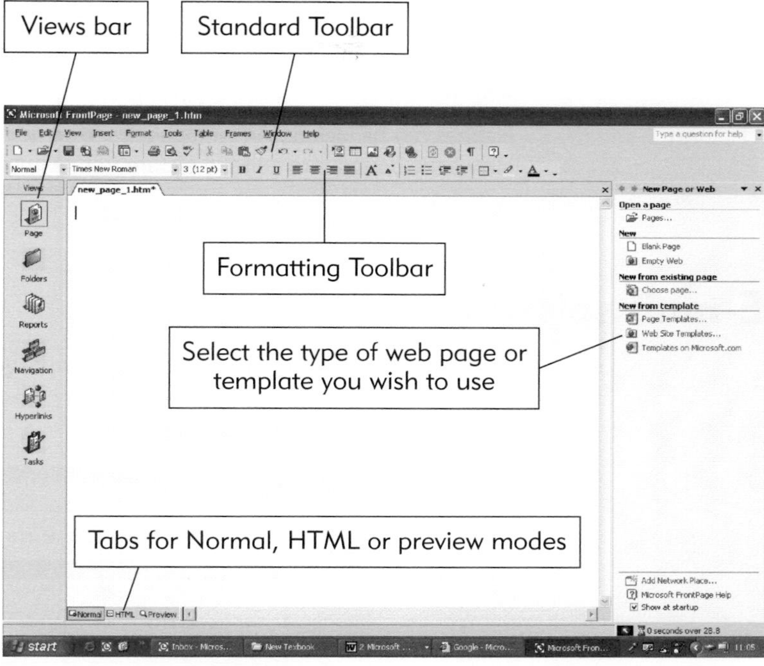

Figure 1.2 Microsoft Frontpage

Feature	Description
HTML pages	All web creation tools allow users to create HyperText Mark-up Language pages. This is the language used for web pages.
Hyperlinks	A hyperlink is a picture or text which when clicked links the user to another web page. All web creation tools allow users to create links.
Different views of the web page	A web designer can look at the web pages in Normal (design) view, in HTML view or in Preview mode. HTML view will show the language code only. Design view lets the user add text and pictures to the page. Preview mode opens the page in a web browser and lets the user see what it will look like when it is opened on the Web.
Navigation	Web creation tools manage the navigation layout of the website. This is shown as a picture, indicating how each page is linked to the other pages in the website.
Tables	Tables can be added to web pages. Most packages have a Tables option where the table properties can be set.
Frameset	A frameset is a group of pages which can be set as one page. The frameset may have a left-hand page and a top page, as well as the main page for text. Although each page is saved separately the frameset makes the pages look like a single page in a web browser.
Text	Web creation tools allow different fonts, styles, colours and effects to be selected for text.

Feature	Description
Marquees	These are scrolling text areas which continuously scroll across the web page giving a dynamic effect. The user can set the timings of the scrolling.
Themes	These come in the form of templates whereby the user can select a given theme for their website.
Pictures	Pictures can be included in web pages and some packages have a picture toolbar which allows the designer to edit the picture from within the web page.

E-mail software

- All e-mail software packages have similar features.
- The table below illustrates some common features of e-mail packages.

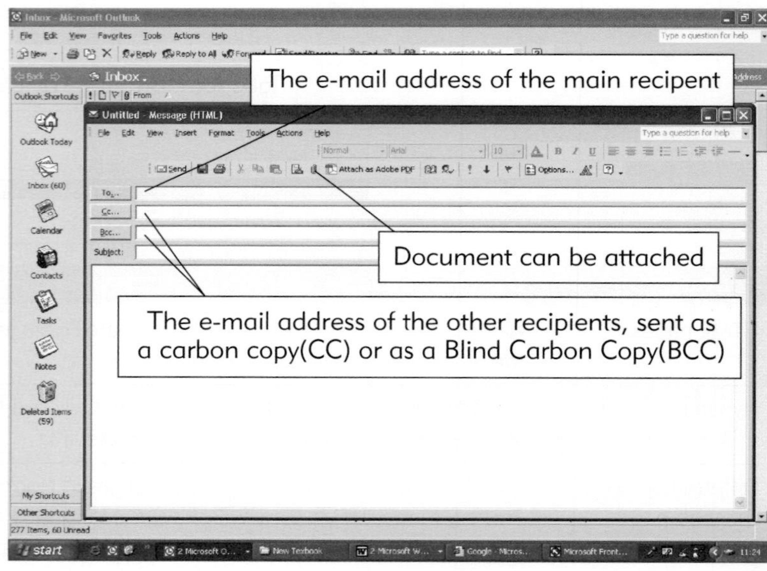

Figure 1.3 Microsoft Outlook

When you send an e-mail to someone, it first goes to your Internet service provider (ISP), from where it is then sent on to that person's ISP. It stays there until the person logs on to the ISP. It then goes to the computer to be read.

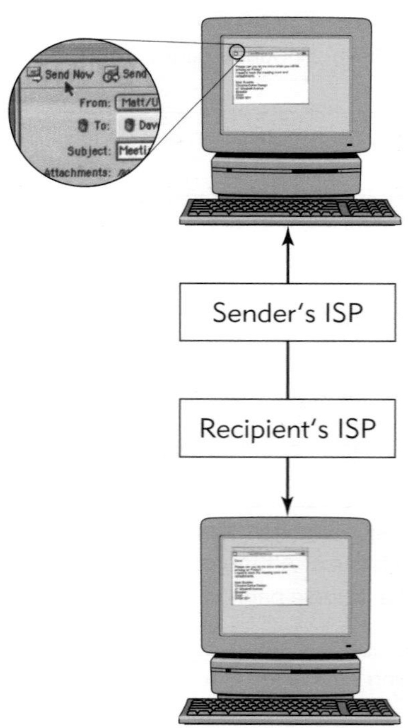

Figure 1.4 Communication by e-mail

Feature	Description
Inbox	Displays all e-mails that have been sent to you. These can be arranged by date, alphabetical order and so on.
From, To and Subject Boxes	Allow you to enter relevant e-mail addresses and a title for your message.
Textbox	Used to enter the message text.
Address button	Allows you access to your electronic address book where you can store all your contacts.
Distribution list	You can also create distribution lists of your contacts so you can send group e-mails.
Attachment button	Allows you to send copies of files such as text, graphics, sound clips or video clips with your e-mail.
Forward button	Allows you to send (forward) an e-mail you have received to another contact.
Reply button	Allows you to reply to an e-mail without having to enter the e-mail address and the subject. These will be done automatically.
Date and time	The computer automatically enters the date and time on each e-mail allowing the user to view e-mails by date sent or even the time sent on a given day.
E-mail signature	The user can create a signature with their details which can be automatically added to e-mails they send.
Digital acknowledgements	Acknowledgements can be automatically sent to sender when the message is read by the recipient.
Priority messages	Priority messaging can be used to allow messages to be allocated different priorities.

Word processing software

- All word-processing software packages have similar features.
- The table below illustrates some common features of word-processing packages.

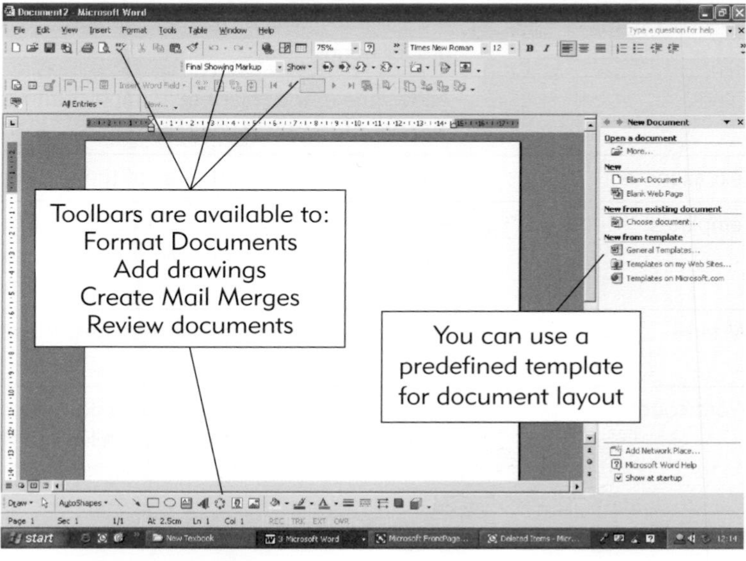

Figure 1.5 Microsoft Word

Feature	Description
Cut, copy, paste, move	Allow the user to edit. Cut allows the user to select and remove text. Copy allows the user to select and copy text which can be placed in another part of the document. Paste allows the user to insert text which has been copied or cut from a document and is temporarily stored on the clipboard. Move allows the user to cut selected text from one place and immediately place the text in another part of the document.
Bullet points	Allow the user to place and format bullet points to assist in presenting their document or creating lists.
Drawing tools	Allow the user to add simple graphics to their documents such as arrows, predefined shapes and boxes.
File format	Allows the user to save documents in different formats, such as RTF, which can then be transferred to other word-processing or publishing packages.
Fonts	Allow the user to select a font type, size and style. Fonts can also be formatted in different colours.
Footer/header	Used to place titles, page numbers, dates etc. in a document.
Grammar checkers	Some word processors can check grammar, although they are limited by the complexities of the English language.
Import clip art/files	Places graphics in documents from other sources, such as files downloaded from the Internet, pictures transferred from a digital camera, or scanned hard copy images.
Mail merge	Combines name and address details, normally imported from a database, with a standard letter. The end result is a set of personalised letters.
Online help	Allows the user to search using a keyword/topic for help. There are usually hypertext links to websites for detailed help.
Print preview	You can see the page before printing – WYSIWYG.
Spell checker	A built-in dictionary. The user can add their own words to the dictionary such as proper nouns.
Tables	Allows the user to place text/graphics into cells in a table. The user decides the number of rows and columns.
Text alignment	The user can select part or all of the text and align it left, right, centre or justify.
Templates	Provide the framework of a document, such as a business letter, that can be repeatly used to provide style consistency so the user does not need to worry about layout. The user simply adds text to predefined positions on the document.
Wizards	Provide step-by-step guidance to help the user perform the more complicated tasks.
Word count	Counts the number of words in a document. This is useful for an essay/coursework where there is a limit to the number of words.

Desktop publishing (DTP) software

- DTP software contains many of the features available in a word-processing package.
- The table below illustrates some common features of DTP packages.

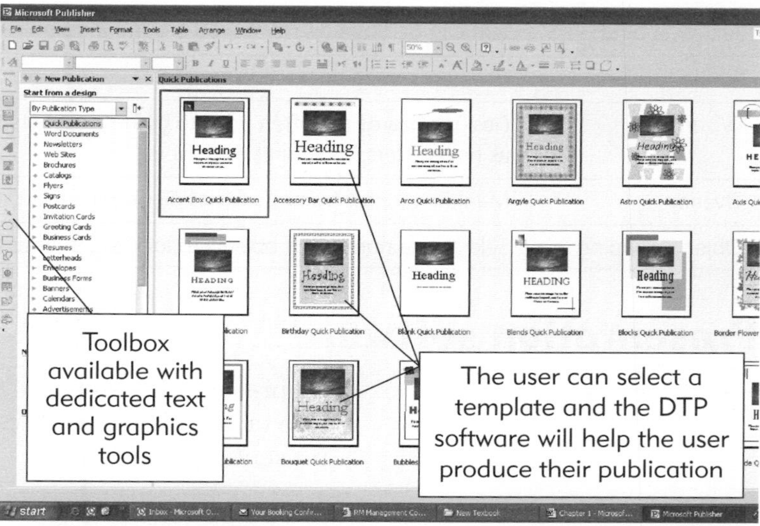

Figure 1.6 Microsoft Publisher

Feature	Description
Spell checker	Built-in dictionary to check spelling. The user can add their own words to the dictionary.
Template/style sheets	The framework of the document is provided for you. This is intended to suit a variety of uses.
File format	Allows you to save your documents as RTF for example so they can then be transferred to other packages.
Text formatting	Font types, sizes, styles, colour.
Drawing tools	Allow the user to produce arrows, shapes, boxes etc. without the need for a graphics package.
Tables	Allow the user to place text in a table. The user can control the format of a table including the number of rows and columns.
Auto contents page	Automatic creation of a contents page using subtitles from the pages created.
Footer/header	Used to place titles, page numbers, date etc. on either the top or the bottom of each page.
Import text/graphics	Text/graphics can be imported from another package in a variety of formats.
Kerning	Adjusting the text spaces between characters. Text modes include normal, expanded and condensed spacing.
Text frames	Allow text to be entered into a text frame.

Feature	Description
Text columns	Users can set up pages for a given publication as a number of text columns.
Picture formatting	Pictures are placed into picture frames, where they can be resized, edited, cropped, etc.
Cropping and scaling	Cropping an image trims the image so that it is more attractive or better fits the available space. Scaling an image increases or decreases the image size to better fit the page.
Text wrapping	Text can be flowed or wrapped around a graphic.
Frame borders	Line borders can be placed around frames. Also graphic borders can be placed around frames.
Wizards	Design wizards are often used to guide a user step by step in creating documents such as newsletters, brochures and flyers.
Overlay	Manipulation of frames such as picture over text, text over picture.
Object grouping	Selecting a number of objects to lock together as one for easier editing.

Presentation software

- All presentation software packages have similar features.
- The table below illustrates some common features of presentation packages.

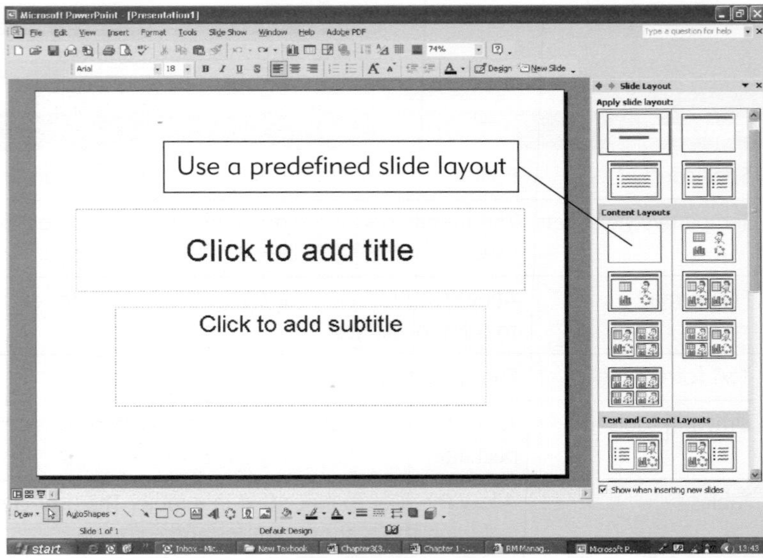

Figure 1.7 Microsoft PowerPoint

Feature	Detail
Slide layout	Allows the user to select a dedicated layout for their slide, such as text in bullet point format with a graphic.
Master slide	The users can create master slides. A master slide is a slide which is used to include features which will appear on every slide. This slide is created only once and can be applied to all of the slides in the presentation.

Action buttons	Buttons that can be placed on your slides to allow an action to be carried out when the user clicks on the button, such as 'go to home slide'.
Timing	Timing can also be added so that the presentation will play automatically without intervention.
Slide effects (animation and transition)	Once you have created your slides, you can control how each slide replaces the previous one. The default is a simple cut from one slide to the next. You can set the transition effect to suit your needs such as 'text flying in from the right'.
Notes page	The user can create a notes page for each slide to add more text for the purpose of a presentation.
Import clip art/files	Places graphics on documents from other sources, such as clip art downloaded from the Internet, pictures transferred from a digital camera ,and scanned graphics from hard copy sources.
Sound and video	Sound clips and video clips can be incorporated to enhance a presentation.

Graphics software

- All graphics software packages have similar features.
- The table below illustrates some common features of graphics packages.

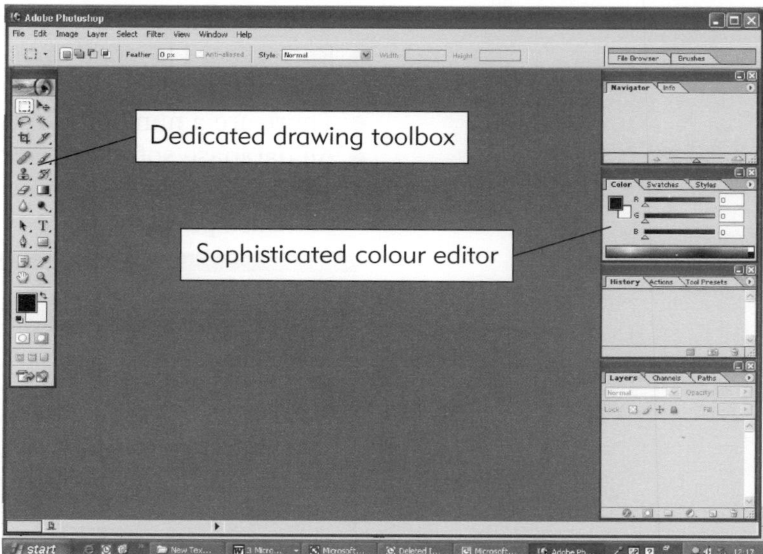

Figure 1.8 Adobe Photoshop

Features	Description
Draw lines	Lines can be straight or curved or they can be drawn freehand by the user.
Predefined shapes	Shapes such as rectangles, circles etc. can be selected by the user.
Size/Scaling	The user can change the size of the shape of graphics as required. This is called scaling.

Features	Description
Cropping	Cutting out part of an image or editing a predefined shape.
Stretch	A shape can be stretched horizontally or vertically.
Rotate/flip	A shape can be rotated through an angle either clockwise or anticlockwise. It can also be reflected horizontally or vertically.
Colour	The user can edit the colour of lines and objects with a paint palette.
Fill	Areas can be filled with shading or patterns.
Zoom	Allows an area of the screen to be seen more closely thus allowing the user to edit detail, such as changing the colour of a pixel.
Clip art	Graphics software often includes a built-in library of drawings and images which can be incorporated in a user's work.
Tool palette	Uses icons to show tools available, such as a brush or a magnifying tool.
Text boxes	Text can be added to an image and edited in the same way as word-processed text.
Save	Graphics can be saved in different formats such as jpeg for web images.

Database software

- A database package allows users to collect and structure data. Data is held in records.
- Each record is made up of fields and each field has a data type.
- There are a number of records in a single table.
- All database software packages have similar features.
- The table below illustrates some common features of database packages.

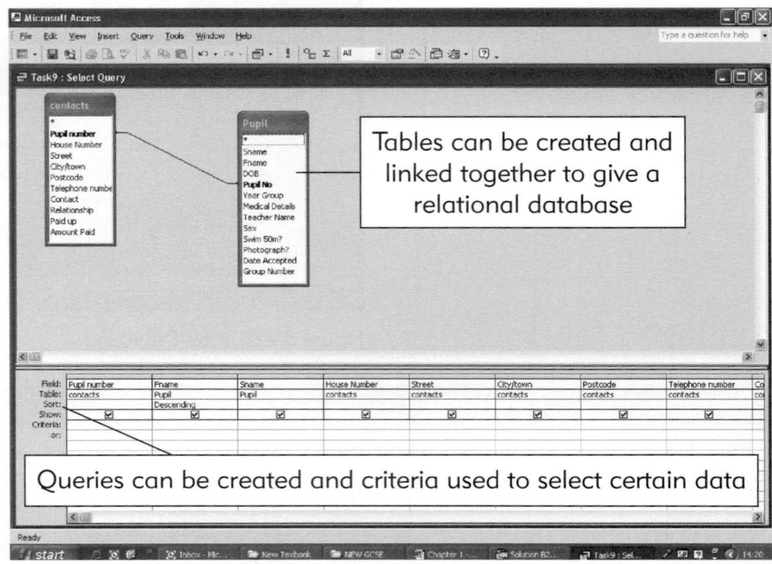

Figure 1.9 Microsoft Access

Feature	Description
Table	A file can be created as a table allowing each field to be defined. The field definition includes aspects such as a field name, data type and field length. The user can also indicate the field that is to be used as a primary key.
Adding, deleting and updating records	The user can add new records, delete old records or change data in a given field within their table(s).
Sorting data	Data can be sorted in either ascending or descending order using one or more fields.
Validation checks	Most database packages can carry out some automatic validation such as checking the data type entered by the user. The user can add further validation checks such as range checks.
Queries	Allow the user to find specific information. To do this the user can select fields and apply criteria, such as using comparison operators (>, < etc.) or logical operators (true or false).
Form design	The user can create forms to capture data on-screen. This can be useful as the form only allows one record to be viewed at a time. If you do not have forms designed all the data is displayed as a datasheet which can make it difficult to see a record.
Report design	Results of queries are usually presented in a table format, but the user can design a report which allows the user to control and decide the way in which the information is presented.
Creating relationships	Tables can be linked together using relationships. This cuts down on the amount of data which has to be stored and makes searching and sorting data more efficient. It also eliminates redundant and inconsistent data.

Spreadsheet software

- All spreadsheet software packages have similar features.
- The table below illustrates some common features of spreadsheet packages.

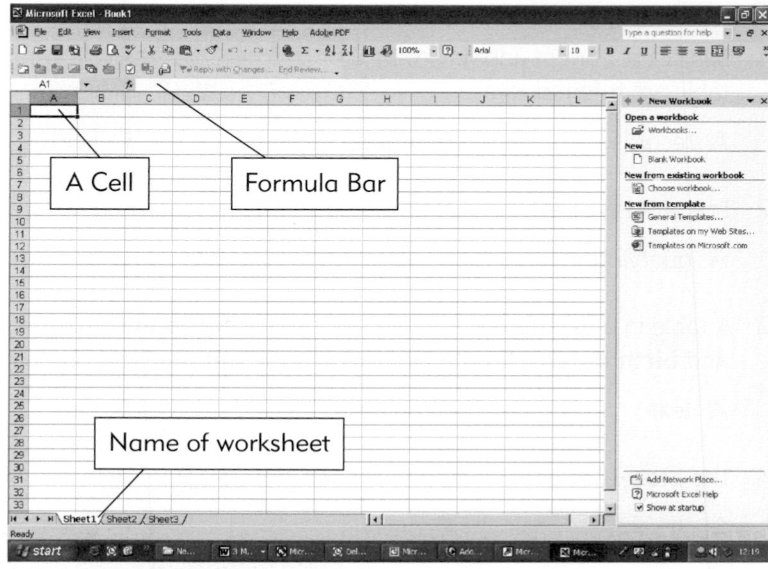

Figure 1.10 Microsoft Excel

Feature	Description
Cell	Cells can hold data in the form of text, number, date, formula or reference to another cell.
Cell format	Cells can be formatted by changing font size and style. Also cells can be given borders or shaded to emphasise appearance. You can also format data in cells, such as a date can be formatted to DDMMYY.
Columns and rows	The user can vary the width of columns and alter the height of cells.
Locking cells	Cells can be protected (read only) which means the user cannot change the data. Cells can also be hidden to assist in security.
Fill	A formula or value can be entered into a cell and can be automatically replicated down or across.
Mathematical functions	The user can select from a choice of built-in mathematical functions. Some of the common functions include SUM, AVERAGE, MIN and MAX.
Graphs and charts	Data entered in the spreadsheet can be displayed as a graph or chart. The user can choose a 2-D or 3-D image and can also select from a variety of chart types. Once the user has selected the data to be displayed the computer will automatically draw the chart.
Conditions	This is an advanced feature which allows the user to create a condition and control possible actions by using an expression such as: IF (condition) THEN (action) ELSE (action)
Lookup tables	Another advanced feature is a Lookup table. These tables contain data that can be continuously referenced using a 'look up' function The function can use Vlookup (vertical look up) or Hlookup (horizontal look up).
Macros	Some experienced users can write small programs called macros. The user creates a series of commands that can be performed automatically by the spreadsheet.

Revision questions

1 Select the correct answer (A, B, C or D) to each of the following questions. Categories of data in a table are referred to as:

A records B groups C fields D files

2 The process of extracting information from the database using a set of criteria is called:

A querying B updating C sorting D merging

3 A table in a database is to have fields called **forename**, **surname**, **age**, **gender**, **phone number** and **birth date**. The data type used in the **gender** field is either **m** or **f**. This data type is called:

A text B numeric C date D Boolean

4 The process of combining information from a database into a word-processed document is called:

A copying B pasting C querying D mail merging

5 Red or green lines appear under words in my word-processed document. This is because:

A text should be in bold
B spelling or grammar errors have possibly been made
C formatting is incorrect
D the font is not recognised by the software.

6

	A	B	C
1	4	9	=Average(A1:B1)
2	5	6	
3	3	7	
4	2	4	

When the formula in C1 is filled down, the answer in C4 will be:

A 13
B 30
C 3
D 6

7 A series of commands and functions that can be run automatically within a spreadsheet is called a:

A macro
B formula
C function
D wizard

8

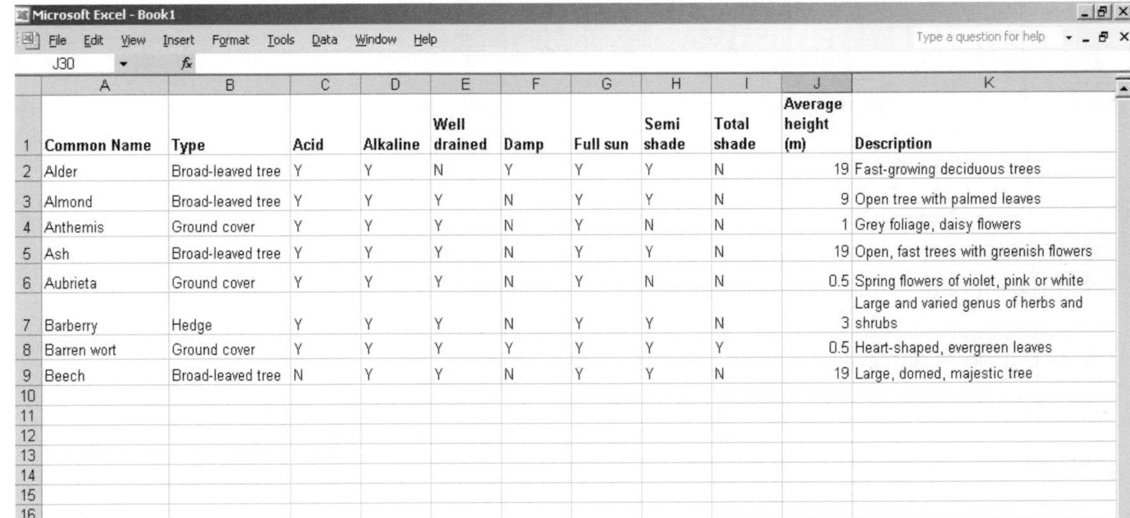

Microsoft Excel - Book1

File Edit View Insert Format Tools Data Window Help

J30

	A	B	C	D	E	F	G	H	I	J	K
1	Common Name	Type	Acid	Alkaline	Well drained	Damp	Full sun	Semi shade	Total shade	Average height (m)	Description
2	Alder	Broad-leaved tree	Y	Y	N	Y	Y	Y	N	19	Fast-growing deciduous trees
3	Almond	Broad-leaved tree	Y	Y	Y	N	Y	Y	N	9	Open tree with palmed leaves
4	Anthemis	Ground cover	Y	Y	Y	N	Y	N	N	1	Grey foliage, daisy flowers
5	Ash	Broad-leaved tree	Y	Y	Y	N	Y	Y	N	19	Open, fast trees with greenish flowers
6	Aubrieta	Ground cover	Y	Y	Y	N	Y	N	N	0.5	Spring flowers of violet, pink or white
7	Barberry	Hedge	Y	Y	Y	N	Y	Y	N	3	Large and varied genus of herbs and shrubs
8	Barren wort	Ground cover	Y	Y	Y	Y	Y	Y	Y	0.5	Heart-shaped, evergreen leaves
9	Beech	Broad-leaved tree	N	Y	Y	N	Y	Y	N	19	Large, domed, majestic tree
10											
11											
12											
13											
14											
15											
16											

The database extract shown has:

A 8 fields and 11 records
B 8 records and 12 fields
C 8 records and 11 fields
D 7 fields and 12 records

9 In what way is the data under the heading **Acid** in Q8 likely to be formatted?

A text
B number
C Boolean
D Date

10 There are over 500 plants in the database in Q8. The manager wants to search for plants that grow in damp conditions to an average height of at least 10 metres. Which of the following criteria could be used to find the data required?

A Damp="y" AND Ave Height (m) ="10"
B Damp="y" AND Ave Height (m) <"10"
C Damp="y" AND Ave Height (m) =>"10"
D Damp="y" AND Ave Height (m) >"10"

Answer true or false to each of the following questions.

1 A primary key is a field that uniquely identifies a record in a table.

2 A one-to-many relationship means that one record in a given table can relate to many records in another table.

3 Combining a word-processed document with records in a database is called mail merging.

4 Sorting a database can only be done using one field.

5 Data redundancy refers to data that has been replaced by updated data.

6 Experienced users find that using a combination of keys is a quicker way of entering instructions.

7 A master slide is the best way to insert a background colour on all slides.

8 A hit counter on a website is referred to as a web component.

9 Bcc is used on an e-mail to let other people see that you have received the e-mail.

10 jpeg is an appropriate form of graphics for use on a web page due to the small storage capacity required.

Match the correct word to each statement

A flat file
B database
C relational database
D bitmap
E data integrity
F compression
G record
H form

1 A view used in databases to view one record at a time.

2 Another name for a row of a database table.

3 A collection of files related to a particular subject.

4 A number of tables that are linked together.

5 This ensures that the data remains reasonable and accurate.

6 Made from a series of small dots known as pixels.

7 Making a file smaller before it is transmitted.

8 Data is stored in a single table and this table has no relationship to any other table.

Examination questions

1 Modelling is a technique used on a computer system. A computer model is:
A a computer program that behaves like real life
B a spreadsheet
C an object on the screen
D a formula CCEA 2002

2 The quickest way to access a web page is to:
A use a search engine with a single word
B use a search engine with a collection of words
C use a meta search engine
D type in the full web page address

Use the following spreadsheet to answer Questions 3–9. It contains the accounts for the tuck shop at a youth club.

	A	B	C	D	E	F
1	**Item**	**Selling price**	**Initial number in stock**	**Number sold**	**Remaining number in stock**	**Value of stock sold**
2	Chocolate	£0.37	60	12	48	£4.44
3	Fizzy drink	£0.49	49	16	33	£7.84
4	Crisps	£0.29	65	24	41	£6.96
5	Mints	£0.36	32	7	25	£2.52
6	Orange	£0.45	25	6	19	£2.70
7	Chewing gum	£0.52	75	30	45	£15.60
8	Total value of stock sold					£40.06

CCEA 2002

3 The format of the cells B2:B7 is:
A Date
B Text
C Currency
D Number

CCEA 2003

4 Cells A8:E8 have been:
A copied
B merged
C validated
D deleted

CCEA 2003

5 The formula used to calculate the value of E2 is:
A C2*D2
B C2+D2
C C2-D2
D C2/D2

CCEA 2003

6 The formula used to calculate the value of F8 is:
A SUM(F2:F7)
B SUM(F2:F8)
C SUM(B7:E7)
D SUM(B2:B7)

CCEA 2003

7 The cells in row 1 have been formatted as:
A Text, centered, bold
B Text, centered, italic
C Text, left, bold
D Text, right, italic

CCEA 2003

8 If the contents of cell B2 is changed to £0.39 the other cells that will change are:
A E2 and F8
B F2 and F8
C D2 and F8
D C2 and F8

CCEA 2003

9 If the contents of cell D6 is changed to 16, the other cells that will change are:
A E6, F6 and F8
B C6, E6 and F8
C E6, E7 and E8
D C6, E6 and F6

CCEA 2003

10 John surfed the Internet to get ideas before he designed his own website. A piece of software used to view pages on the Internet is best described as:

A a navigator
B a browser
C an explorer
D a searcher

CCEA 2004

11 A pupil is preparing a curriculum vitae (CV) for a Record of Achievement (ROA) folder. He decides to use one of the wizards that are available on his word processor.

Curriculum Vitae

Jack Jones
123 High Street
New Town
Co Armagh
BT35 6XY

Interests
I am interested in badminton and football and support my local team. I enjoy listening to music and going out to the cinema. I am a member of the youth club in the town. I attend the Debating Society in school.

Examination Grades I obtained the following grades in my mock GCSE examinations:
English C, Maths B, Science C, ICT A, French D, Geography B

Other information
I have a part job in the local supermarket where I work on the check out. I help out with paper deliveries on a part-time basis.

a Why is a wizard suitable in this case?
The finished document looks like the one shown above.

b The pupil wants to improve the appearance of paragraph 2, the Examination Grades. Describe how he could do this.

c The pupil wants to change the order of the paragraphs so that paragraph 1 comes after paragraph 2. Describe how this could be done.

CCEA 2003

12 A weekly newspaper is produced using a desktop publishing (DTP) package.

a One feature of a DTP package is text wrap. Explain what text wrap means. Use a diagram if it helps.

b Give three other features of a DTP package that makes it suitable for newspaper production.

CCEA 2003

13 A school library database contains records about books and pupils. Three files or tables are used as shown below:

Book	Pupil	Borrows
Book_Id	Pupil_Id	Pupil_Id
ISBN	Surname	Book_Id
Shelf_Code	First_Name	Date_Out
Title	Year	Date_In
Author	Form_Group	
Subject		
Publisher		

The librarian uses commands to search the book file, for example:

SELECT Book
LIST Title, Shelf_Code
FOR Title CONTAINS "Belfast"

would list the **Title** and **Shelf_Code** for all books in the file that have the word **Belfast** in the book **Title**.

SELECT Pupil
LIST Surname, First_Name
FOR Year EQUALS 8

would list the names of all pupils in Year 8.

Write commands similar to those in the examples to:

a list the **Title** and **Shelf_Code** for all books by the author **PD James**

b list the names of all pupils in form group **9RT**.

CCEA 2003

14 A search engine is used to find information on the Internet. Some search engines use keywords or phrase searching.

a Why is the user likely to get more relevant results if a phrase or combination of words is input in the search?

b The user sometimes has the choice of making the search case sensitive. What does case sensitive mean?

c With simple queries the user is often allowed to use a wildcard. For instance Alta Vista's wildcard is an asterisk (*). If a user entered **foot*** in the search box, give three results they might obtain.

d Logical or Boolean operators are often used when searching the Internet. Name two logical operators.

e Explain how logical operators might be used to find the names of all the hotels and guesthouses in Armagh.

CCEA 2003

15 Graphic packages usually have tools to enable the user to carry out various tasks. Explain when each of the following might be used in the creation of a drawing.

a Pre-defined shapes.

b Freehand drawing.

c Text creation and manipulation.

d Copy and paste.

e Colour palette.

CCEA 2003

16 A school secretary is asked to produce a personalised letter to every teacher in the school. She will store the teachers' details in a database.

a It has been decided to use the mail merge facility provided by the word processor. Describe how the secretary will use the mail merge facility to produce her letters.

b The school secretary often has to send letters to parents about, for example, school trips, parent–teacher evenings, Year 8 induction details etc. She has decided that she could make use of templates.

i What is a template?

ii List two advantages to the school secretary of using templates.

CCEA 2003

17 A company keeps a database with two tables. The tables are **Supplier** and **Part**. The structure of the tables is shown below:

Supplier Table	**Part Table**
Supplier Code	Part Number
Supplier Name	Supplier Code
Street	Description
Area	CostPrice
Town	SellingPrice
Postcode	InStock
Telephone	OnOrder

Here is some data from each of the tables.

Part Table

Part Number	Supplier Code	Description	CostPrice	SellingPrice	InStock	OnOrder
DEC001	BLA100	Twin Tip Deck	£6.65	£8.50	0	Yes

Supplier Table

Supplier Code	Supplier Name	Street	Area	Town	Postcode	Telephone
BLA100	Back & Sons	23 Long Road	Bangor	Co.Down	BT22 OEU	02800706050

a Suggest a key field for the:
  i Part Table
  ii Supplier Table.

b The files are held in a Relational Database. Explain the term Relational Database.

c Explain why the **Supplier Code** is in the **Part Table**.

CCEA 2004

18 Browser software can be used to view pages on the Internet.

a Name two web browsers.

Users can return to their selected homepage by clicking on an icon similar to this. 

b Name four other icons you would expect to find on a browser menu bar.

CCEA 2004

2

Unit C2: Understanding of ICT systems in everyday life

C2(a) Knowledge of ICT components

In this section you will learn about the components of an ICT system. Every computer system is made up of input, output, storage and processing devices. Each of these components work together and form a system which can process data and present information.

Acronyms and abbreviations

Acronym/abbreviation	Meaning
CPU	Central Processing Unit
VDU	Visual Display Unit
CD-ROM	Compact Disk – Read-Only Memory
DVD	Digital Versatile Disc
RAM	Random Access Memory
ROM	Read-Only Memory
bit	Binary Digit
MB	Megabyte
GB	Gigabyte
LCD	Liquid Crystal Display
dpi	Dots Per Inch
OCR	Optical Character Recognition
SVGA	Super Video Graphics Array
ppm	Pages Per Minute
CD-R	Compact Disk-Recordable
CD-RW	Compact Disk-Rewritable
WORM	Write-Once Read-Many
GUI	Graphical User Interface
WIMP	Windows, Icons, Menus, Pointers

Identify component parts of a typical home PC

A typical home computer has a Central Processing Unit (CPU – also called the processor), input devices (e.g. keyboard, mouse), output devices (e.g. monitor), storage devices (e.g. hard drive).

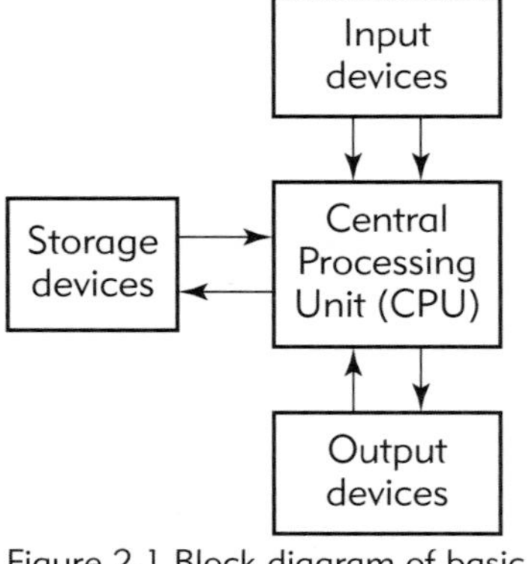

Figure 2.1 Block diagram of basic computer

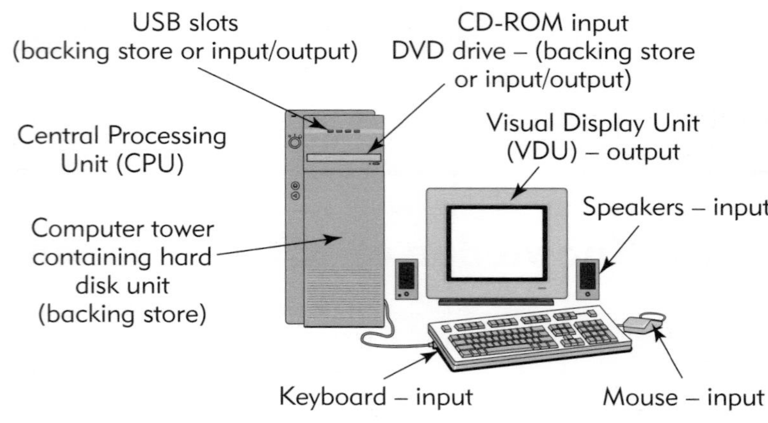

Figure 2.2 Desktop PC

You should be able to label all parts of this diagram and state the function of all the components.
The components form a system and are related, as shown above.

What is the CPU?

All processing of data occurs here. Processor speed is in gigahertz (GHz). Typical processor speeds start at 1GHz.
The processor is made up of:

- Control unit – which co-ordinates the Input and Output devices and all related activities.
- Arithmetic and Logic Unit (ALU) – Calculations are done here and logical decisions are made.
- Main memory – which holds the programs and data that are currently being used.

Operating systems

The operating system enables all of the hardware and software to work together. It also allows the user to interact with the computer system.
Windows Vista and Windows XP are operating systems. The operating system of a computer is stored on the hard disk whilst the computer is switched off.
The operating system will:

- share time between processes and applications running on the computer

- allocate memory effectively so that all processes have an adequate amount of memory to run
- manage and communicate with all devices connected to the computer – this is sometimes done using driver software
- provide a user interface for the user to communicate with the computer – the most popular type of interface is a Graphical User Interface (GUI).

The Graphical User Interface (GUI)

A GUI uses **Windows**, **Icons**, **Menus** and **Pointers** (WIMP) so that the user can interact with the computer.
Through the GUI of the operating system the user can perform tasks, such as creating folders, deleting files, creating shortcuts to programs, installing software, examining the contents of a disk drive, setting desktop properties and many other things.

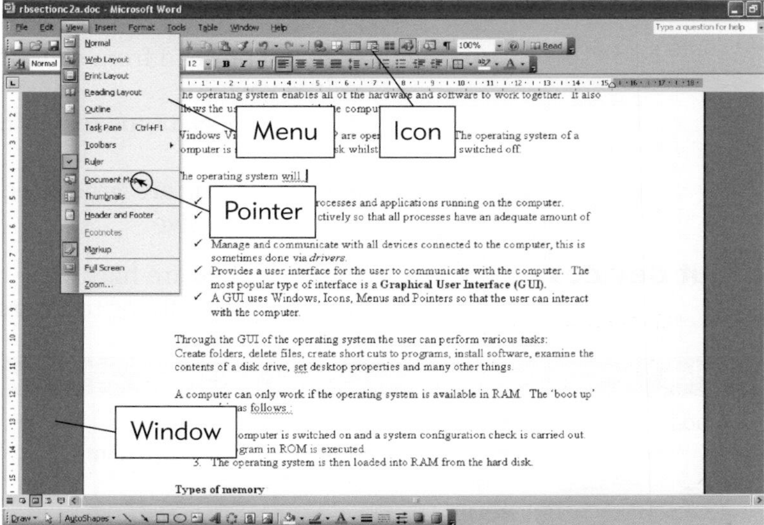

Figure 2.3 You can see the window, a menu, icons and a pointer.

A computer will only work if the operating system is available in RAM. The 'boot up' sequence is as follows:

1. The computer is switched on and a system configuration check is carried out.
2. A boot strap program held in ROM is executed, this tells the computer to load the operating system.
3. The operating system is then loaded into RAM from the hard disk.

Types of memory

The CPU contains different types of memory.

RAM (Random Access Memory)

- It can be read from or written to.
- It is volatile – that is the contents of the memory are lost when the machine is switched off.

- It is used to hold programs and data that the user is using, for example Microsoft Windows, Microsoft Word and the document being typed.
- Typical RAM size is up to 1 GB.
- The amount of RAM can influence the performance of the computer.
- More RAM can improve the speed at which data is processed.

ROM (Read Only Memory)

- It can be read from but not written to.
- ROM is non-volatile – that is programs stored on ROM are permanent and the contents cannot be altered.
- It is used to store the 'boot up' program for the operating system. This program runs automatically when the computer is switched on to load the operating system.

Cache memory

- It can be read from or written to.
- It is volatile.
- It is a special type of fast memory located close to the processor.
- Instructions are processed faster when in cache memory.
- It is expensive.

Input devices

Input devices are hardware components which can be used to enter data into or to interact with the computer system.

Device	Features	Advantages/Disadvantages
Keyboard	• Has a standard QWERTY layout. • Used to enter large amounts of text into the computer. • Used on tills, remote controls and at most ATMs. These keyboards may have fewer keys with emphasis on numeric keys. Concept keyboards are special keyboards which have keys with pictures or words. For example, they are used in supermarket fruit and vegetable departments for customers to weigh their own purchases. They are also used on vending machines.	• The speed of input depends on the human operator. • Can be slow compared with other input devices. • Prone to human error since all data is entered 'by hand'. Concept keyboards provide 'shortcuts' for users who do not have to be specially trained to use them.
Mouse 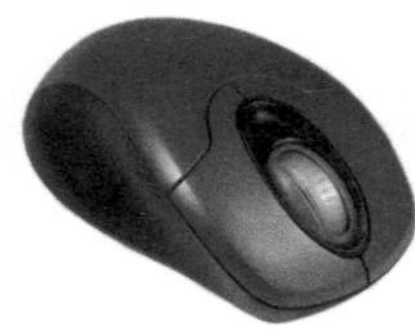	• Also referred to as a 'pointing device'. • Designed to fit under the hand. • When it is moved a pointer on the screen moves in the same direction. • A ball moves and built-in sensors pick up the movements and send corresponding	• Easy to use. • Inexpensive compared with other input devices. • Experienced users may find using a mouse slow compared with using 'hot keys'. For example they might

Device	Features	Advantages/Disadvantages
Mouse *Cont.*	signals back to the computer. • Can have two or three buttons which are used to make selections on the screen. • Can be wireless using infrared or other wireless technology. • A tracker ball is an alternative to a mouse.	prefer to use Ctrl+P to print rather than selecting menus and options.
Joystick	• Allows the user to control the movement of the cursor on the screen by moving a small lever in different directions. • Usually has buttons that allow actions to be carried out. • Used to play computer games (in this context it may be referred to as a **games paddle**). • Used to move computer-controlled devices such as robots and hospital scanners.	• Easier to use than a mouse. • Can be expensive – more expensive than a mouse. • A light touch on the joystick gives speedy input.
Tracker pad	• Also known as a touch sensitive pad. • Used as an alternative to a mouse on a laptop computer – the pad can sense the touch of a finger. • Movement on the pad allows control of the cursor which in turn allows the user to select menu options and icons. • Double tapping a pad is the same as double clicking a normal mouse button.	• Very sensitive and therefore, at first, can be more difficult to use than a mouse. • Can lose sensitivity. • Easily damaged because the surface is made of a fragile material. • Devices using this type of technology are usually more expensive. • Less mobility is required to use a pad than a mouse or joystick.
Microphone	• Inputs analogue sound into a computer where it is converted to a digital signal. • When used as part of a voice recognition system the signals can be converted to text or used as commands to control the computer or other systems.	• Voice recognition can be successful when a user 'trains' the computer to recognise their voice by storing words and phrases. • Voice recognition is helpful for users with less mobility. They can use their voice instead of a mouse or other input device. • Also records background noise. • Relatively cheap.
Digital camera	• Stores pictures on a memory card. • Memory cards have a capacity up to 1 GB which allows around 400 pictures to be stored in medium resolution or quality. • Most have a small liquid crystal display (LCD) screen which can show stored pictures, including that just taken. • Most digital cameras can capture short video clips that last a couple of minutes.	• Can store many more pictures than can be taken using a cartridge of film. • Pictures can be edited or deleted on the camera. • Pictures can be uploaded and/or edited directly on the computer. • Pictures can be emailed. • Pictures can be viewed on the LCD screen and retaken immediately if needed.

Device	Features	Advantages/Disadvantages
Digital camera *Cont.*		• Pictures can be printed immediately and cost less than film processing. • Pictures may not be as good a quality as those taken by conventional cameras. • Sometimes digital cameras can be more expensive than conventional cameras.
Scanner	• Converts a hard copy of pictures or text to a digital image. • Works by passing beams of bright light over the image. The image is recognised as a large number of dots on a page. • The quality of the image scanned is measured in dots per inch (dpi). • Cheap scanners can scan at 2400 dpi but only up to A4 in size. • Hand-held scanners are portable and can be used to scan barcodes for stock taking in a supermarket. • 3-D scanners use laser light to produce a 3-D model of a subject.	• Once the image has been scanned it can be saved and changed using standard software. • If text has been scanned it can be recognised as text on a word processor using optical character recognition (OCR) software. • The quality of the scanned image is dependent on the resolution of the scanner.
Touch screen	• A special type of screen which reacts to human touch. When a user's finger touches the screen, vertical and horizontal beams of light are broken. The touch position is found by detecting which light beams have been broken. • Used in conjunction with GUIs. • Used in banks, tourist offices, museums and information kiosks. • Also used on hand-held games consoles, PDAs and mobile phones.	• User does not require much ICT competence compared with using a mouse or a keyboard. • More expensive than normal screen. • May lose sensitivity.

Output devices are hardware components used to present information from a computer.

Device	Features	Advantages/Disadvantages
Dot matrix printer	• Impact printer – print head strikes the paper through an ink ribbon. • Print head is made up of a series of pins laid out in rows and columns. • Characters made up of dots are formed on a page when the tiny pins strike the ink ribbon. • The more pins in the print head, the better the quality of the printer.	• Useful when organisations need to produce carbon copy printouts such as invoices or delivery notes. • Costs less to produce multiple copies of data (using the carbon copy method). • Cheaper to run than other printer types. • Slower at producing output than other printer types. • Print quality is low. • Can be noisy.

Device	Features	Advantages/Disadvantages
Laser printer **Printer resolution** is the sharpness of text and images on paper. It is measured in dots per inch (dpi).	• Non-impact printer – uses powder toner to produce images on a page • Powder toner is transferred to the page to form images or letters. The toner is fused permanently to the page using heat and pressure. • Some laser printers can print in colour. • Some laser printers are combined with scanner, photocopier or fax capabilities. • Suitable for high volume printing. • Usually have their own memory where pages are temporarily stored before printing. • Mainly used on school networks, offices and at home.	• High resolution – typically 1200 × 1200 dpi so print quality is excellent. • Fast – typically prints 26 pages per minute (ppm). • Very quiet. • Cheap to run as toner cartridges last a long time. • Expensive to buy. • Complex to repair. • Can take up a lot of space.
Ink-jet printers 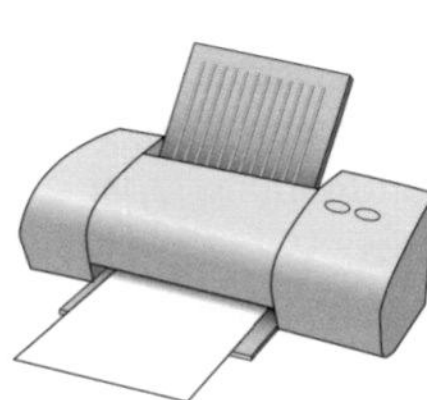	• Non-impact printer – uses black and coloured ink cartridges to create images on a page. • Print head contains tiny nozzles. The ink is heated and then sprayed through the nozzles to form characters or images.	• Good quality output, some give photo quality output. • Cheap to buy. • Expensive to run as cartridges are expensive and run out quickly. • Printing slower than a laser printer. • Ink can smudge. • Small, lightweight and portable. • Suitable for printing photographs and small number of pages.
Plotters 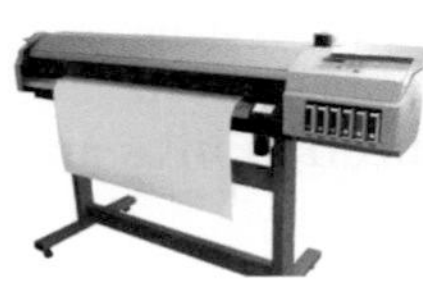	• Can be flat-bed or drum. • Draws highly accurate diagrams using a fine electronically-controlled pen. • Example uses are to draw plans, line diagrams and electrical circuit diagrams. • Used by architects, surveyors, pattern makers and engineers.	• Can use large paper sizes. • Drawings are high quality. • Can draw arcs or curves. • Can draw characters of different sizes and different fonts. • Multicoloured pen sets are available so that graphs of different colours can be drawn. • Slow at producing output. • Not suitable for text output. • Expensive to buy.
Monitors 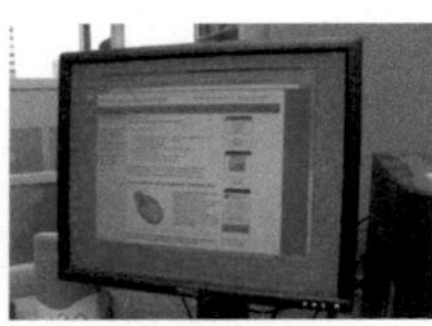	• Displays information from the computer on the screen. • Picture is made up of thousands of tiny dots called pixels. • Typical screen size is 17 inches from corner to corner. • Typical screen resolution is 1024 × 768 pixels. • VGA (Video Graphics Array) resolution (640 × 480) is used in PDAs and pocket PCs.	• VDUs (Visual Display Units) or desktop monitors use a cathode ray tube (CRT) and work in a similar way as a television. They take up a lot of space. • TFT LCD (Thin Film Transistor Liquid Crystal Display) monitors are much lighter and smaller than a typical desktop monitor. They use less power than CRT monitors by using LCD technology to create pixels. These

Device	Features	Advantages/Disadvantages
Monitors *Cont.* A **pixel** is the smallest part of a digital **image**. **Screen resolution** is a measure of the quality of the image on the screen. The more pixels the higher the resolution. The higher the resolution the better quality the image will be on screen.	• SVGA (Super Video Graphics Array) resolution (800 × 600) was used in many PCs. • XGA (Extended Graphics Array) resolution (1024 × 768) is now widely available for PCs. • The cost of the monitor increases with size and resolution.	monitors are better for users in terms of health and safety. • TFTs give off less heat than a CRT monitor. • TFTs are easily damaged by sharp objects. • Some multimedia monitors have speakers and a microphone built in. • Many different sizes are available, for example PDAs, laptops and desktop computers have different screen sizes. • One disadvantage of monitors is that there is no permanent copy of what is on screen.
Speakers	• Provide sound output through the sound card from a computer. • Can be built-in (e.g. as in a laptop) or they can be attached to the computer.	• Allow an audience to listen to sound associated with multimedia presentations or films. • Can be useful for visually impaired users. • Can be distracting if used in public places or a classroom.

Storage devices

Storage devices permanently store data or information. Memory and storage on a computer is measured in **bits** and **bytes**.

- A bit (or binary digit) is the smallest unit of storage on a computer. It is a 1 or 0.
- 1 byte = 8 bits (a character is usually 8 bits in size).
- 1 kilobyte (kB) = 1024 bytes
- 1 megabyte (MB) = 1024 kB
- 1 gigabyte (GB) = 1024 MB

Magnetic storage devices

Hard disk

- Consists of a number of rigid disks stacked on top of one another.
- Data is stored on tracks and sectors.
- Typical capacity 100 GB.

- Each disk surface on the stack has a set of read/write heads making data transfer much faster than floppy disk or Zip drive.
- The hard disk drive is contained in a sealed unit to protect it against damage from dirt and dust.
- A typical hard disk is built in the computer system, this type of disk is not portable.
- Internal hard disks are used to permanently store the operating system, all software and user data on a PC or network.
- Hard disks are much more expensive than any other type of magnetic media.
- **External hard disks** are also available. These are portable with a high storage capacity. They can be attached using a USB or Firewire connection and are suitable for small-scale backup of data.

Zip disk

- Medium capacity form of a floppy disk using floppy disk technology.
- Typical capacity up to 250 MB.
- Uses read/write heads on the Zip drive to retrieve and save data, although the transfer time is faster than the ordinary floppy drive.
- Zip disks are thicker and slightly wider than floppy disks but are still portable.
- Larger capacity makes them suitable for storing large files, for example multimedia presentations.
- Zip drives can be internal or external to the computer.
- A Jaz drive uses hard disk technology and can store up to 2 GB. Data transfer is faster than the Zip disk. It is suitable for data backup on a PC.

Magnetic tape streamers

- A device which reads and writes data stored on magnetic tape.
- Magnetic tape has a typical storage capacity of 70 GB.
- Data is stored in blocks and there is a gap between each block.
- Transfer of data is slow because magnetic tape uses serial access (for example if a file is stored on block 15, blocks 1 to 14 must be read first).
- Most networks have a tape streamer linked to the server, which uses magnetic tape to archive/backup data everyday.
- Magnetic tape is a cheap way of storing a large amount of data.

3.5 inch floppy disk

- Circular plastic coated disks with a magnetised surface. The disk must be formatted before use.
- Data is stored on tracks and sectors on the disk.

- Capacity 1.44 MB.
- Uses read/write heads inside the floppy drive to retrieve and save data. This can be slow.
- Can be easily damaged if exposed to high temperatures or magnetic fields.
- Floppy disks are portable but the small capacity means they can only be used to store small documents or files.
- Newer computers do not have floppy drives so they may be used less and less.

Optical storage devices

Optical disks are plastic disks that are similar in size to a music CD. Data is burned onto the surface of the disk using a laser beam which makes small indentations known as pits.

Compact Disk (CDs)

- Typical capacity 700 MB.
- Data transfer speed is high. The speed of data transfer is limited by the speed at which the disk can be spun in the drive. For example 8 × spins a disk at 4000 rpm (revolutions per minute).
- CDs are portable and not as easily damaged as floppy disks.

CD-ROM (Compact Disk – Read-Only Memory)

- These disks are purchased containing data.
- When the user receives the CD, data can be read from it but NOT written to it.
- Used to store music, software, encyclopaedias.
- The cost of a CD-ROM is determined by the nature of the data stored on it.

CD-R (Compact Disk – Recordable)

- These disks are purchased blank (empty).
- The user can record data onto the disk ONCE only. This is known as WORM (Write-Once Read-Many).
- Data can be read from the disk as often as required.
- CD-Rs are used to store data, music or for small-scale backup from a PC.
- CD-Rs are relatively cheap.

CD-RW (Compact Disk – Rewriteable)

- These disks are purchased blank (empty).
- CD-RWs can be written to, erased and rewritten many times.
- CD-RWs are more expensive than CD-Rs.

DVD (Digital Versatile Disk)

- Look like ordinary CDs.
- Are encoded differently to CDs and so need a different drive (a DVD drive) to read them.

- A DVD drive can usually read CDs too.
- Typical storage capacity 4.5 GB Single Layer up to 17.5 GB Double-sided Dual Layer.
- Used to store large quantites of data and feature films.
- Could be used for back-up purposes.
- DVDs are more expensive than CDs and the data transfer rate is faster.
- DVDs can be read from and written to and the following types are available:
  - DVD+R – once writeable DVDs.
  - DVD-RW – rewriteable DVD, but the whole disk has to be erased each time data is written.
  - DVD+RW – rewriteable DVD, data can be added and removed without erasing the whole disk and starting over again.

Flash storage devices

Flash devices use flash memory, which is electronically programmed, to store data. They have become the main portable storage device used by pupils.

Flash memory facts:

- It is non-volatile.
- It can be erased.
- It has no moving parts.
- It is used in memory cards, USB Flash drives, PDAs and mobile phones.

Figure 2.4 Flash memory device

USB Flash drive facts:

- Use Flash memory integrated with a USB interface.
- The USB Flash drive must be plugged into the USB port of the computer to be active. This connection forms the power supply.
- Capacity for USB Flash drives is 32 MB – 2 GB.
- The larger the capacity of the USB Flash drive the more expensive it will be.
- Data transfer is faster than floppy technology.
- More compact, holds more data and is more reliable and durable than other portable memory because there are no moving parts.
- Are also called USB Flash pens.

Revision questions

1 Copy the following table. Expand the acronyms/abbreviations and give a short explanation of what each one is.

Acronym/abbreviation	Expansion	Explanation
CPU		
VDU		
CD-ROM		
DVD		
RAM		
ROM		
bit		
MB		
GB		
LCD		
dpi		
OCR		
SVGA		
ppm		
CD-R		
CD-RW		
WORM		
GUI		
WIMP		

2 Anne is going to buy a new computer. Explain to her the role of each of the following components in a computer system.

a RAM
b ROM
c CPU

3 Complete the following paragraph using each word only once.

kilobyte byte bit character

A ______ is the smallest unit of memory. Eight bits make up one ______.

A ______ is usually one byte in size. A ______ is made up of 1024 bytes.

4 List these units on order of size

kilobyte byte megabyte gigabyte

5 A computer has a Windows operating system.

a What is the function of the operating system in any computer?
b List three tasks performed by the operating system of a computer.
c Describe three functions of a GUI which make it suitable for use by novice users.

6 Outline the boot up sequence for a PC.

7 Fill in the blanks using each word only once.

volatile	non-volatile	operating system
read-only memory	random access memory	

RAM stands for ______ ______ ______. This type of memory is ______, which means that all data is lost when the computer is switched off.

ROM is ______ ______ ______. This type of memory is ______, which means that data is retained after the computer is switched off. The ______ ______ is loaded in RAM when the computer is started up.

8 Select the statements which are true.

Statement	Tick if true
RAM cannot be written to.	
Data in ROM is not lost when the computer is switched off.	
RAM can be written to but not read from.	
RAM can be written to and read from.	
ROM holds the operating system.	
ROM holds the program which boots up the computer.	

9 What is the function of **cache** in a computer system?

10 Select appropriate input devices for each of the following tasks.

Purpose	Device
Entering large amounts of text into a computer.	
Playing computer games.	
Using a GUI.	
Weighing fruit and vegetables in a supermarket.	
Converting hard copies of pictures into digital images.	
Selecting options on a screen in a tourist information office.	
Moving the mouse cursor on a laptop.	
Recording voice input for storage on a computer.	

11 A scanner can be used to create digital images from photographs. Give one other use for a scanner and explain how it can be used.

12 List three input devices you might find in a supermarket and explain how they would be used.

13 a A touch screen is used:

A to input large amounts of text
B to print large amounts of text
C to select options instead of a keyboard
D to select options instead of a printer

b The most suitable output device for printing carbon copies is:

A a laser printer
B a dot matrix printer
C an ink-jet printer
D a VDU

c A laser printer prints on a page using:

A a ribbon
B toner
C liquid ink
D multicoloured pens

d Which of the following is NOT a disadvantage of using a plotter:

A slow plotting output
B unsuitable for text output
C produce low quality drawings
D expensive

e Which statement about screen resolution is true?

A It depends on the physical size of the screen.
B It depends on the number of pixels on the screen.
C The fewer pixels the better the resolution.
D The smaller the physical size of the screen the better the resolution.

f Which statement about laser printers is untrue?

A They are high resolution printers.
B Print quality is excellent.
C They produce output very quickly.
D They are very noisy when printing.

g An inkjet printer would be best used for printing:

A 30 000 high quality letters
B a GCSE geography project
C a set of architect's plans
D a carbon copy invoice for a customer

14 Copy and complete the table below by stating which printer you would consider to be best for each task and listing two features which make the printer suitable for the task.

Task	Printer	Two features
30 000 high quality letters		
A GCSE geography project		
A set of architect's plans		
Producing a carbon copy invoice for a customer		

15 List three differences between a TFT screen and a cathode ray VDU.

16 What is the main function of backing storage devices?

17 Re-order the following list by typical capacity, smallest first.

floppy disk   magnetic tape   CD-RW   Zip disk   Hard disk

18 Copy and complete the following table.

	CD-R	CD-RW	CD-ROM
Capacity			
Purchased blank?			
Can be written to many times?			
Is used for?			
Cost			

19 Which storage device would you recommend for backing up a school network? Give two reasons for your choice.

20 List three magnetic storage devices and state which has the fastest data retrieval time.

21 List three optical storage devices and state which has the highest storage capacity.

22 Describe the main features of Flash memory. List three ways in which it can be used.

Examination questions

1 **a** A CD-ROM can be:

A written to but not read from
B written to and read from
C read from but not written to
D neither written to nor read from

Answer _______ [1]   CCEA 2007

b A floppy disk is an example of:

A a magnetic storage device
B an input device
C an optical storage device
D an output device

Answer _______ [1]   CCEA 2007

2 Consider the following printers. Tick TWO boxes that apply for each printer.

a Dot matrix printer
- ☐ Has a print head which contains many nozzles.
- ☐ Prints pages at a high speed.
- ☐ Is an impact printer.
- ☐ Print head strikes paper through a ribbon.
- ☐ Is a non-impact printer.
- ☐ Is used to produce architect's plans.

[2]

b Laser printer
- ☐ Has a print head which contains many nozzles.
- ☐ Prints pages at a high speed.
- ☐ Is an impact printer.
- ☐ Print head strikes paper through a ribbon.
- ☐ Is a non-impact printer.
- ☐ Is used to produce architect's plans.

[2]

c Plotter
- ☐ Has a print head which contains many nozzles.
- ☐ Prints pages at a high speed.
- ☐ Is an impact printer.
- ☐ Print head strikes paper through a ribbon.
- ☐ Is a non-impact printer.
- ☐ Is used to produce architect's plans.

[2]

d Ink-jet printer
- ☐ Has a print head which contains many nozzles.
- ☐ Prints pages at a high speed.
- ☐ Is an impact printer.
- ☐ Print head strikes paper through a ribbon.
- ☐ Is a non-impact printer.
- ☐ Is used to produce architect's plans.

[2]

3 Mike is going to buy the following computer system, but he cannot understand the descriptions in the bullet point list.
- Intel Pentium D 820 processor
- 2.8 GHz, 800 MHz FSB, 2 MB cache
- Microsoft Windows XP operating system
- 1 GB DDR RAM
- 160 GB hard disk
- Dual layer DVD Rewriter
- 128 MB ATI X1300 graphics
- 802.11g Wireless Network Ready
- 19 inch flat-panel monitor – high resolution

a Give Mike an explanation of the following terms:
- **i** hard disk drive [2]
- **ii** processor [1]
- **iii** DVD rewriter [2]
- **iv** resolution [2]

b The shop assistant has mentioned that the computer system above also has some software supplied and has ROM.
- **i** What software is supplied with the computer?
- **ii** What is the main purpose of ROM in a computer?

[2]

c Mike decides to buy some extra software. Which software would be most suitable for each task he has to do? (Tick **ONE** for each task, the first one has been done for you.)

[4]

Task	Word processor	Spreadsheet	Database	Presentation software
Storing details of his CD collection			✓	
Planning his spending over the next three months				
Preparing his history coursework report				
Storing names and addresses for his Christmas card list				
Preparing information to give a talk to members of a local golf club				

CCEA 2007

d Mike is going to buy a printer, a scanner and a microphone. List **ONE** item of hardware and **ONE** item of software that he will need to ensure the printer works with the computer.

[2]

CCEA 2007

4 Martina wants to buy a new entertainment PC and has found the following one in PC Universe.

- 2.8 GHz processor
- 2 MB cache
- Microsoft Windows XP media centre
- 1024 MB RAM
- 4 GB ROM
- 400 GB hard disk
- Multiformat dual layer DVD RW drive
- Wireless keyboard and mouse
- 32 inch HD-ready LCD TV

a Microsoft Windows is a GUI. What does GUI stand for?

[1]

b Name **TWO** features of Microsoft Windows that make it user friendly.

[2]

c Why does an entertainment PC need a 400 GB hard disk drive?

[2]

d Look at the specification and categorise all the memory types as volatile or non-volatile memory types in the table.

Volatile memory types	Non-volatile memory types

[3]

e Tick the correct definition of cache memory in the table.

Definition	Tick
Stores the largest instructions used in processing	
Stores most frequently used instructions	
Stores data currently being processed	
Stores recovered files when programs do not respond	

[1]

f When Martina starts up her PC the boot-up program is loaded into main memory from ROM. What does the acronym ROM stand for?

[1]

CCEA 2006

C2(b) Information systems

This section is for students taking the Full Course only. In this section you will learn about collecting, checking and storing information and data. Validation and verification techniques are defined and the importance of data portability is demonstrated. The advantages of storing data in a relational database as opposed to a flat file are also discussed.

Abbreviations

Abbreviation	Meaning	Explanation
ASCII	American Standard Code for Information Interchange	A standard code made up of a set of binary digits and representing a letter.
OMR	Optical Mark Recognition	A scanner is used to scan text on a document into the computer. OCR software on the computer changes the letters into characters that can be edited on a computer.
OCR	Optical Character Recognition	A scanner is used to scan marks on a specifically designed document into the computer. OMR software changes the marks into meaningful data so that the computer can process it.

You will need to know about the following file extensions and the features of files stored in each of these formats.

csv gif jpeg mpeg rtf tiff pict

Information and data

Data is raw facts and figures which have not been given a meaning.

Here is a set of data: 43 67 56 89 45 77 90

Information is data that has been processed and given a meaning.

Teacher Mark Sheet

Subject: Maths Class: 9B

Teacher: Mrs Black

Name	**Mark (%)**
John Jones	43
Mary Smith	67
Anne Cleese	56
Hannah Greer	89
Giles Clarke	45
Alan Gray	77
Mark Black	90
Average Mark	67%

Data can be processed by a computer system to produce information.
Data is input through an input device, then processed or changed in some way and the information is output to a screen or on paper.
The data has now become information. Thus the list above is now a set of exam marks for a class and the average mark has been calculated.

Collecting data for processing

Data must be collected on a form before being processed by a computer. A well-designed form will help ensure that the data collected is correct and complete. Information created from correct and complete data is more likely to be of high quality. A form should include:

- a title suitable for the purpose of the form
- a logo representing the company collecting the data
- a prompt which represents each item of data to be collected
- a suitable space to enter each item of data – the space can be on a line or in the form of a box, tick box, radio button, etc.
- instructions on how to fill out the form
- a brief explanation which clearly explains the purpose of the form.

When designing a form think about font, colour and positioning of items:

- The font chosen should be suitable for the intended audience.
- The font should vary in size to emphasise section and headings.
- The colour should be used to enhance the form where appropriate, for example to break down into sections.
- Images, such as company logos, should not obscure areas of the form.

Forms can be paper-based or screen-based.

Figure 2.5 Screen-based form

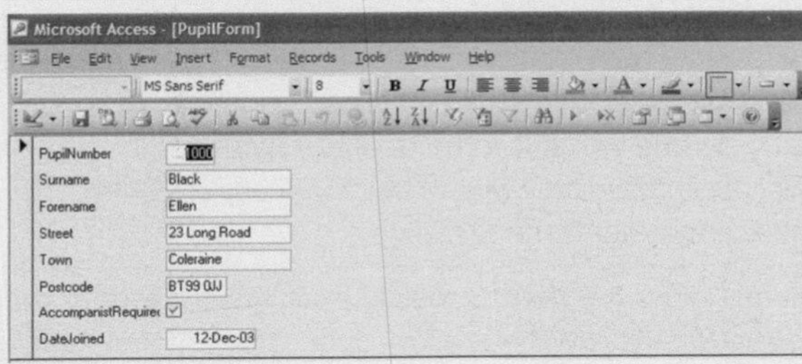

Microsoft Access - [PupilForm]
File Edit View Insert Format Records Tools Window Help
MS Sans Serif 8

PupilNumber	1000
Surname	Black
Forename	Ellen
Street	23 Long Road
Town	Coleraine
Postcode	BT99 0JJ
AccompanistRequire	☑
DateJoined	12-Dec-03

Figure 2.6 Paper-based form

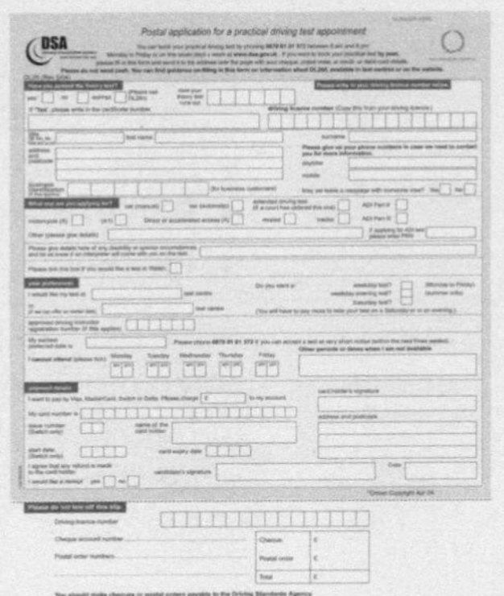

Data checking

Verification

When data is collected on paper it must be entered into the computer by an operator before being processed. To ensure that the data has been entered correctly we use **verification**. The process of verification involves comparing two versions of the data entered and detecting any differences, then correcting data where appropriate.

Methods of verification

- Proofreading
  - Typed documents can be proofread to ensure that they contain correct and accurate information.
- Double entry of data
  - The same data is keyed into the computer by two different computer operators.
  - The computer system compares the two sets of data.
  - Any mismatching data is rejected and must be re-entered.

Validation

Data collected using a data-entry screen must be checked, by the software, before it is accepted by the computer system. Checking data to ensure that it is acceptable and sensible is called **validation**.

Methods of validation

Validation of data ensures that the data is present, of the correct type, in the correct range and of the correct length.

Validation check	Purpose
Presence	A presence check will ensure that data has been entered into an area on the form. This check means that data which must be entered is not omitted.
Length	A length check will ensure that data entered is of the correct length.
Type	A type check is used to ensure that the data entered is of the correct format. There is a range of data types. When defining data we usually give it a type and a valid range. Examples of data types are: • **Numeric** – data takes on a numeric value and such data can be used in calculations. • **Text** – data can be made up of letters, or letters and numbers. • **Date** – data takes on a value which is formatted as a date. • **Boolean** – data which can have only two values, normally yes or no. • **Currency** – data which represents money values.
Format	Some database packages allow the user to specify exactly what format the data being entered should take. The database will not allow data to be entered in any other format. For example, a **Supplier Code** field might be assigned an input mask that requires three letters followed by three numbers to be entered – 'ABC123' is accepted but '123ABC' is rejected.

Validation check	Purpose
Range	A range check ensures that data entered is within a given range. For example: ● a customer number can take on values between '1' and '500' ● pupil grades can take on values between 'A' and 'E'.
Lookup tables	Lookup tables or lists hold valid values for data. When data is entered the lookup table is checked to ensure that the data is within the allowable list. These can be used very successfully in spreadsheet applications.

Check digit

Figure 2.7 An ISBN barcode

A check digit is a character which is added to the end of a code. The check digit is compared with the results of a calculation on the code. If the results of the calculation do not match the check digit, the code has to be input again. The ISBN barcode on a book is a good example of where check digits are used. They are also found at the end of the Universal Product Code (UPC) or barcode on items in supermarkets.

Data capture

Validation and verification help to minimise human error. Direct data capture is where data is read directly into a computer rather than typed in. Two examples of this are Optical Mark Recognition (OMR) and Optical Character Recognition (OCR).

Method	Advantages	Disadvantages
OMR ● Scans forms which have been filled out using marks or ticks. ● Uses light to detect the position of the marks on the form. ● Used on the National Lottery tickets and multiple choice exams. Figure 2.8 An OMR form	● Fast – inputting large amounts of data can be done quickly so many documents can be processed one after the other. ● Accurate – eliminates the possibility of typing errors because data is read directly from a document. ● OMR data can be analysed by the computer to produce high quality information quickly. ● Staff will need minimal training to use the system because documents are simply passed into a scanner.	● Expensive – the cost of buying OMR equipment and producing specially designed forms can be high. ● OMR documents must be kept in good condition – the system may not be able to read creased documents. ● Not an environmentally friendly solution – forms should be recycled after input.

Method	Advantages	Disadvantages
OCR • Reads handwritten or typed documents and turns them into digital characters. These can then be processed by a computer. • A document scanned using OCR can be edited digitally. An ordinary scanner will have an OCR function –. this means a hard copy of a typed document can be scanned and then edited in a word processor. • Used by the Royal Mail to sort the post. The system reads the postcode written on letters and routes the letter.	• Fast – large quantities of text can be input to a computer quickly • An electronic copy of a paper-based document can be created without retyping it • Handwritten data (like a postcode) can be processed directly by a computer without having to key the data in.	• Documents which are not in good condition or are marked will not be read accurately. • Expensive to buy systems which are highly accurate. • Will not always produce accurate results when required to scan forms (especially with boxes and check boxes), very small text, shady photocopies, mathematical formulae, handwritten text.

Data structure: Flat files and relational databases

Data stored on ICT systems is stored in files. Files can be made up of **records** and these are made up of a number of **fields**. Each field has a **data type**, for example **text**, **currency**, **numeric**.

A **file** (called a **table** in a database) is a collection of records.

A **record** is a unit of data which is made up of a number of fields. There is one record per item in the database.

A **field** is the smallest single piece of data in a file. Fields can hold different types of data.

Flat files

The following data is held in a flat file database.

A flat file database looks like a spreadsheet. The data is organised into rows and columns but there are no relationships linking tables.

Figure 2.9 A flat file database with four records and seven fields.

	A	B	C	D	E	F	G
1	Pupil ID	Surname	Forename	Subject	Coursework	Examination	Total
2	1000	Black	Anne	French	30	45	75
3	1050	Doherty	Elaine	Spanish	45	48	93
4	1060	Matthews	Richard	Spanish	33	40	73
5	1000	Black	Anne	German	44	45	89

Field name	Data type
Pupil ID	Numeric
Surname	Text
Forename	Text
Subject	Text
Coursework	Numeric
Examination	Numeric
Total	Numeric

Disadvantages of using a flat file

Redundancy

Look at the entry for **Anne Black**. Her name is recorded twice because she studies two languages. Data such as her **Surname** and **Forename** has to be repeated. When data is repeated unnecessarily it is said to be **redundant.** This makes the file much bigger than it needs to be and so searching through it will take more time.
If another entry is made for Anne Black the file would now look like this:

	A	B	C	D	E	F	G
1	Pupil ID	Surname	Forename	Subject	Coursework	Examination	Total
2	1000	Black	Anne	French	30	45	75
3	1050	Doherty	Elaine	Spanish	45	48	93
4	1060	Matthews	Richard	Spanish	33	40	73
5	1000	Black	Anne	German	44	45	89
6	1000	Black	Annie	Spanish	33	44	77

Figure 2.10 Second version of the flat file database

The new entry contains data which is incorrect. Anne Black's forename has been recorded as **Annie**.

Integrity

The more often data has to be recorded the higher the possibility of the data having an error or inconsistency. The correctness, reliability and accuracy of the data is called **data integrity**. Flat files may have a low level of data integrity.

Relational databases

Relational databases can solve the problems posed by flat files. We can create tables which are related.

Facts about relational databases

- They hold data in files or tables.
- The tables are linked together using relationships.
- Relationships are made between fields in the tables.

- Data is organised in a way which makes searching and sorting easy.
- They provide a system for managing access to data.

In order to improve the flat file example above, we can create two tables and relate them.

- One **PUPIL** has many **MARKS**. This means that there is a one-to-many relationship between the two tables.
- The tables are linked on the field **Pupil ID**.

Each time a pupil gets marks for a new subject only their **Pupil ID**, **Subject**, **Coursework**, **Examination** and **Total** will be recorded. Their **Surname** and **Forename** are recorded only once in the **PUPIL** table. This cuts down on data redundancy.

Figure 2.11 A one-to-many relationship.

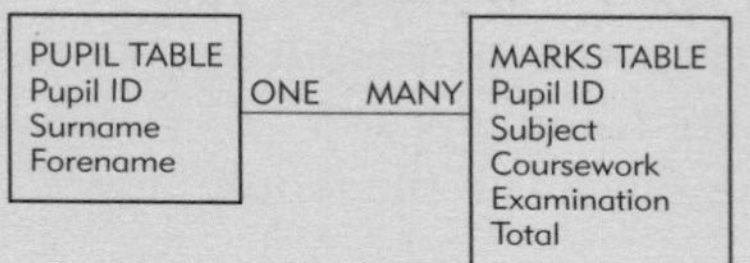

Figure 2.12 This is how the data would look if it was recorded in a relational database like Microsoft Access.

Pupil ID	Surname	Forename
1000	Black	Anne

Subject	Coursework	Examination	Total
French	30	45	75
German	44	45	89
Spanish	33	44	77
*			

Pupil ID	Surname	Forename
1050	Doherty	Elaine

Subject	Coursework	Examination	Total
Spanish	45	48	43
*			

Pupil ID	Surname	Forename
1060	Matthews	Richard

Subject	Coursework	Examination	Total
Spanish	33	40	73
*			

Key terms

- Key field – also called ‘primary key’ – a field whose value will uniquely identify each record in a table.
- Relationship – a link that has been made between two tables using fields contained within both tables.

Advantages of relational databases

- The security of data stored in a single location can be managed more easily.
- Different access privileges can be given to users so that the data can be protected from unauthorised access.
- Repetition of data is minimised so there is little or no data redundancy.
- Searching for data is quicker because there is very little repeated data.

- Most data is recorded only once making it more likely to be correct, accurate and reliable throughout the database.
- Key fields and relationships help ensure data integrity.
- Relationships between files means that data from all tables in the database can be searched at the same time.

Data portability

Data portability is the ability to transfer data from one system or software application to another without having to re-enter the data.
Some file formats are highly portable, that is they can be used in a range of systems or software applications.

File type	Description
CSV – Comma Separated Variable	• A simple text file. Field names are entered first. Each record is entered on a new line. • Can be imported easily into a database or spreadsheet. Date,Time,Temperature 12/12/02,2pm,12 12/12/02,2:30pm,10 12/12/02,3pm,15 12/12/02,3:30pm,19 12/12/02,4pm,9
RTF – Rich Text Format	• Allows users to transfer data between different word processors on different operating systems. • Documents scanned using OCR are usually saved as rtf documents. This means that the document can be opened using a variety of word-processing applications.
JPEG – Joint Photographic Experts Group	• A compressed image file format. • Commonly used on web pages. • Normally small files. • A file stored as a jpeg can be used in any document on a number of different operating systems. • Can be opened in the Windows and Apple Macintosh operating systems, making them highly portable.
MPEG – Moving Picture Experts Group	• Used for moving pictures. • This is a compressed file format.
PICT	• Macintosh native picture format. • They are used by Macintosh graphics applications, supporting high quality images and can be compressed.

File type	Description
TIFF – Tagged Image File Format	• This is a graphics file format and stores bitmapped images. • This format is portable between different applications and different types of computers – it can be used in a Windows and Apple Macintosh environment.
GIF – Graphic Interchange Format	• This graphics file format supports compressed images. • They are usually small in size and are suitable for inclusion on web pages.
• TXT – Text File (also called ASCII text files). Most text files use ASCII (American Standard Code for Information Interchange) codes for characters.	• This is a simple text file which will hold letters and numbers but not formats such as bold and italic. • ASCII files can be imported into a word processor but the ASCII file may not appear in its original format. Each word processor will apply its own page layouts to ASCII files. • ASCII files are highly portable and are supported by almost every application.
MIDI – Musical Instrument Digital Interface	• These sound files are produced when digital musical instruments are connected as input devices to a computer.
MP3	• MP3 music files are CD quality compressed recordings that are about ten times smaller than the equivalent CD WAV/AIFF (Audio Interchange File Format) file. • MP3s are reduced in size by filtering out all noise that is not detectable to the human ear.

Data compression

Data can be compressed for storage or transmission. This means the data will take up less storage space or bandwidth. **Advantage**: Compressing files to a fraction of their original size makes them smaller to send or store. WinZip will compress in this way into ZIP files.
Disadvantage: These files are compressed before being transported and must then be decompressed at their destination before they can be used.

Use data compression:

- to email a large file attachment, reducing the time taken to transmit an email, or so it becomes small enough to fit into a recipient's mailbox
- when a file is slightly larger than the size of a floppy disk, the compression tools can make the file smaller so it will fit on the disk

- to save storage space, as the file can be stored in compressed format.

Many different types of data can be compressed using the correct file format.

- Graphics can be compressed using JPEG or GIF format.
- Music files can be compressed using MP3 format.
- Video files can be compressed using MPEG format.

In all cases the purpose of compression is to make the files smaller in size to aid efficient digital transmission or storage of the data.

Revision questions

1 Expand the following acronyms/abbreviations and give a brief explanation of how each is used in a computer system.

Acronym/abbreviation	Expansion	Explanation
ASCII		
OCR		
OMR		

2 Using a suitable example describe the difference between data and information.

3 The manager of Smalltown Basketball Club needs to collect data about members. The following data needs to be recorded.

Title	
Forename	
Surname	
Sex	
Date of Birth	
Street	
Town	
Postcode	
Phone Number	
Distance from the club	
Method of transport	Can be taxi, bus, car, walk, cycle.
Previous club	Can be a club name or NONE.
Permission to use photographs	Can be yes or no.
Medical Conditions	
Parent's name	

a Create a well-designed paper-based data capture form which will record the required details.
b List four things which you have considered when designing your form.

4 The manager of Smalltown Basketball Club decides to record the paper-based data on a computer. He needs to design a database.

a For each of the fields state which data type would be most appropriate and give a sample value for the field.

Field	Data type	Sample data
Title		
Forename		
Surname		
Sex		
Date of Birth		
Street		
Town		
Postcode		
Phone Number		
Distance from the club		
Method of transport		
Previous club		
Permission to use photographs		
Medical Conditions		
Parent's name		

b The manager decides to add a Key Field to the database. What is the purpose of a Key Field in any database?
c Why would Surname not be a suitable key field?

5 When data is being entered into a computer, it should be validated.

a What is the purpose of validation?
b List three types of validation checks and explain their purpose.

6 Copy and complete the table below. Which validation check would you use in each case?

Task	Validation check
To ensure a surname is less than 30 characters.	
To ensure that a value has been entered in the Key Field.	
To ensure that a date has been entered in the following way: 12/12/99	

To ensure that a postcode has been entered correctly.
To ensure that data entered is a number.
To ensure a membership number is between 1000 and 2000.

7 Verification can be used to check data that has been entered into a computer system. Explain two methods of verification that could be used to ensure the Smalltown data has been entered correctly.

8 How can a check digit be used as a method of verification?

9 What is direct data capture?

10 a Which of the following is a correct statement about OMR?

A It is not suitable for high volumes of data and scans characters from a form.
B It is not suitable for high volumes of data and scans marks from a form.
C It is suitable for high volumes of data and scans characters from a form.
D It is suitable for high volumes of data and scans marks from a form.

b Which of the following is a correct statement about OCR?

A It is not suitable for high volumes of data and scans characters from a form.
B It is not suitable for high volumes of data and scans marks from a form.
C It is suitable for high volumes of data and scans characters from a form.
D It is suitable for high volumes of data and scans marks from a form.

c Which of the following might NOT be defined as data?

A 1, 2, 3, 4, 5, 6
B A, B, C, D, E
C A, 1, B, 2, C
D 12 cm, 14 m, 14 km, 19 mm, 78 m

d Verification can be defined as:

A Proofreading of documents and correction of differences.
B Double entry of information and correction of differences.
C Comparison of two versions of data and detecting differences.
D Proofreading and double entry of the same data.

e Look at the following screenshot.

	A	B	C	D	E	F	G
1	Pupil ID	Surname	Forename	Subject	Coursework	Examination	Total
2	1000	Black	Anne	French	30	45	75
3	1050	Doherty	Elaine	Spanish	45	48	93
4	1060	Matthews	Richard	Spanish	33	40	73
5	1000	Black	Anne	German	44	45	89

Which statement is true?

A There are seven fields and four records.
B There are seven records and four fields.
C There are five records and seven fields.
D There are seven records and seven fields.

f In the screenshot in part e), Pupil ID is likely to have the following data type:

A Text B Numeric C Boolean D Currency

11 A company wants to set up a database of customers and orders. It is thinking about using a flat file. Explain three problems with using flat files.

12 Complete the following using each term once only.

DATA REDUNDANCY RELATIONSHIPS TABLES

RELATIONAL DATABASE DATA INTEGRITY

Using a ______ ______ solves the flat file problem. ______ are used to link ______ together. This avoids ______ ______ and improves ______ ______.

13 What is data portability?

14 John has a multimedia presentation on his home computer. It is 55 MB in size.

a How can data compression help him get the presentation into school?
b What tool could he use to compress the presentation?
c When he gets the presentation onto the school network, how can he open it?
d Give one advantage of compressing data.

15 Which of the following statements are true?

A txt is a graphics file format and gif is a graphics file format.
B midi is a graphics file format and gif is a graphics file format.
C tiff is a graphics file format and gif is a graphics file format.
D csv is a graphics file format and gif is a graphics file format.

16 Explain how a CSV is a portable file in a computer system.

Examination questions

1 "Mobiles 4 Many" cannot decide between a flat-file and a relational database system to keep track of customers and their mobile phone orders.

a Explain to the company why data held in a relational database is generally more secure than in a flat file database. [2]

b Relational databases help maintain data integrity and reduce data redundancy. Explain the terms data integrity and data redundancy. [1]

c The company have decided to use a relational database. They have created the following two tables but cannot decide which field to use to link them together. [1]

Table 1

Customer Number	Customer Name	Address	Home Telephone Number

Table 2

Customer Number	Mobile Telephone Number	Make	Model	Date of Purchase

i Which of the above fields would you use to link the two tables together? [1]

ii Why did you choose this field? [1]

CCEA 2007

2 Check digits help validate the data being entered at the POS. There are many other validation checks carried out in computer systems.

a Explain the purpose of each of the following validation checks.

i Lookup table [1]

ii Type check [1]

iii Length check [1]

b Select the most appropriate validation check for the following data fields. Each check can be used once only.

i Lookup table [1]

ii Type check [1]

iii Length check [1]

Field name	Staff Number	Staff Name	Job Title
Validation check			

c Another method of data checking is verification. What happens during data verification? [2]

CCEA 2007

3 Which one of the following file extensions is not used for a text file format?

A csv **B** rtf **C** txt **D** gif [1]

CCEA 2007

4 A tennis club stores information about members on a database. A small section of the database is shown below.

Member Number	Firstname	Surname	Date of Birth	Gender	Team
1234	Mary	Wilson	12/3/90	F	A
1245	John	Sweeney	19/8/91	M	A
1250	Margaret	Lynas	10/4/87	F	B
1304	Robert	Swann	10/06/91	M	A
1308	Owen	Black	10/06/87	M	B
1305	Pippa	Brunswick	10/05/90	F	B

a **i** Which is the key field in this database? [1]

ii Why is a key field necessary in a database? [2]

iii Give ONE situation where it would be necessary to modify a record in the database. [1]

b The manager of the club wants to be able to search the database. She uses the query feature of the database. This query statement will return the names of all female members.

PRINT Firstname, Surname WHERE Gender EQUALS "F"

i Write down the criteria for this query. [1]

ii Write the query statement which will return the names of all members in team B. [2]

iii What other feature of the database would be useful for presenting information? [1]

CCEA 2007

C2(c) Digital communication systems

In this section you will learn about how digital technology is used to communicate. Computers must be linked together in some way to allow communication. Communication can be over a short distance, perhaps within a building, or across the world. Either way cables or wireless links are required.

Abbreviations

Abbreviation	Meaning
LAN	Local Area Network
WAN	Wide Area Network
ISP	Internet Service Provider
HTML	HyperText Mark-up Language
URL	Uniform Resource Locator
ISDN	Integrated Services Digital Network
PSTN	Public Switched Telephone Network
www	World Wide Web
ADSL	Asymmetric Digital Subscriber Line
PC	Personal Computer
WAP	Wireless Application Protocol

Figure 2.13 A network schematic

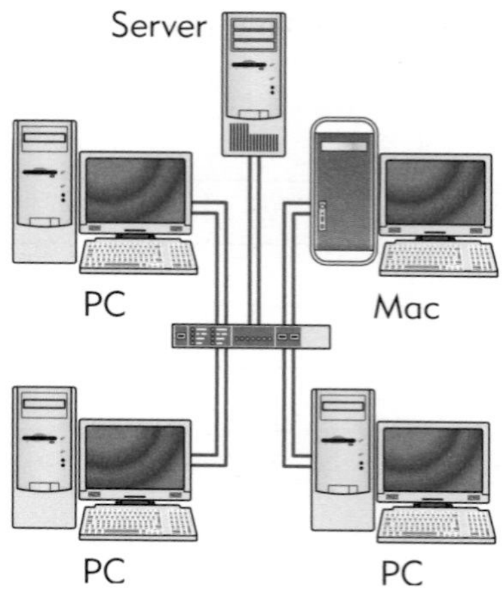

Data networks – LANs and WANs

A network is a set of computers which are linked together.

Local Area Network (LAN)

Features:

- Used in places like schools and offices.
- Spread over a small geographic area such as one or two buildings.
- Links computers in the buildings using network cables or wireless connections.

Advantages:

- Peripherals like printers and scanners can be shared between a number of computers.
- Software stored on the file server can be shared by all the computers on the network.
- Users can share files and work on joint projects using shared resources on the network.
- Users have flexible access, they can log on at any computer and access their files.
- Computers and users can communicate easily using e-mail or conferencing.

LAN components

File server

A file server is the main computer on the network.

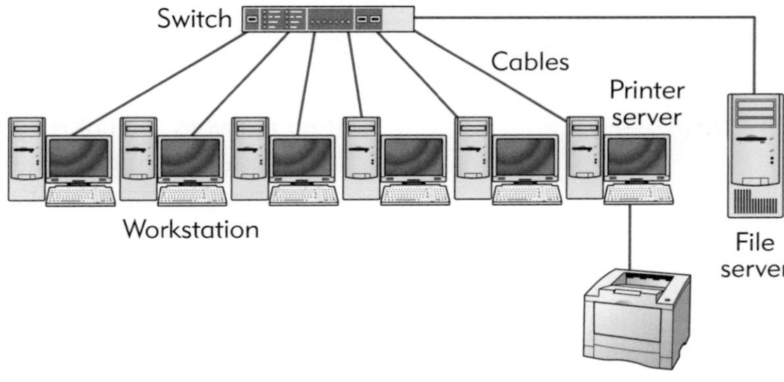

Figure 2.14 A star network

A file server:

- stores the network operating system software, such as Microsoft Windows XP
- stores the application software, such as Microsoft Word
- stores files created by the users of the system
- stores the system software which will manage the network resources and security
- stores the utility software such as a virus checker
- manages communications across the network
- manages security on the network, for example usernames, passwords and access codes ensuring that only authorised users can log on.

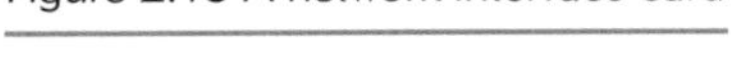

Figure 2.15 A network interface card

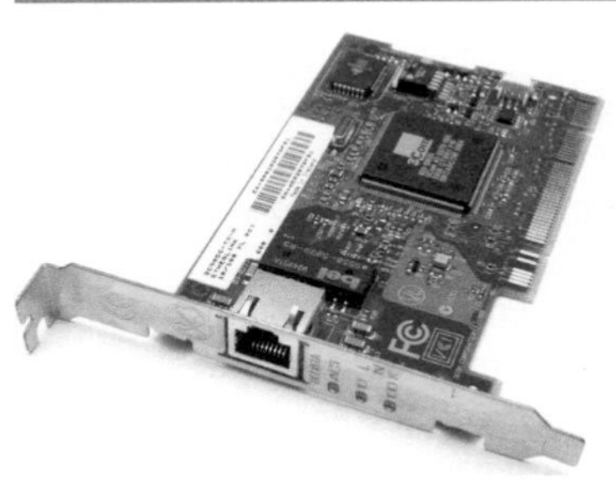

Network interface card

A special piece of equipment which allows the PC to communicate with the network file server and all other computers on the network.

Figure 2.16 Network cable and connector

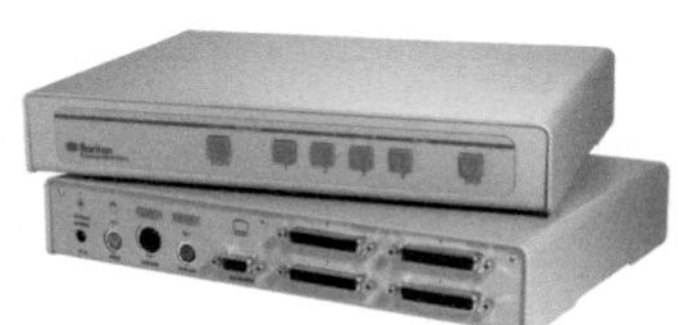
Figure 2.17 A network switch

Network cables

The network cables plug into the back of each computer and link the computers together. These cables plug directly into the network card contained inside each computer.

Switches

A switch is a single connection point for a group of computers. Several computers are connected directly to a switch using network cables.

Network software

Network software must be installed on a computer that is part of a network. This allows it to communicate with the file server and other computers.

Network topology

Networks can be set up in different shapes. This is called the topology of the network. There are three main topologies:

- Ring network – all of the computers are linked together in the shape of a ring. Data travels around the network in one direction, between the computers. If a computer in the ring breaks down or is switched off the network will not be able to operate.
- Bus network – computers or workstations are linked using one main cable, called the backbone cable. The main cable runs along the network in a single line. Each computer is linked to the main cable.
- Star network – these have a central file server and all of the computers are linked via a cable to the main computer. The cable comes from each computer to a switch/hub.

LAN security

Securing the network means protecting the software, user data and computers against damage and unauthorised access.

Protect from:	How?
Unauthorised access by users or hackers	• Give each user a unique username and password. If the password and username do not match the person will not be allowed access to the network. • Use a firewall to protect from unauthorised access via the Internet. *A firewall is software which is designed to prevent unauthorised access from outside a LAN. The firewall may also protect against some viruses and stop certain types of files from leaving the LAN.* • Encrypt data when it is travelling along a network. Encryption is the process of encoding data which is to be sent across a network, making that data unreadable to anyone who intercepts it. Only a user with the encryption key software can read the data when it arrives at its destination.

Viruses (a program or software designed to damage a computer)	• Install virus protection software and keep it up to date. Scan portable storage devices like USB flash drives for viruses. • Filter e-mail and attachments to ensure that viruses are not included.
Authorised users who might damage important files	• Use different levels of access, giving different people different access rights. For example a teacher has more access rights than a pupil.
Unexpected breakdown resulting in the loss of data	• Keep backup copies of data. These can be stored on magnetic tape, on an external hard drive (for a network) or on another portable storage medium (like DVD or CD) for a PC. • Make backups of the system at regular intervals. • In schools and offices a backup is usually taken every day.
Physical damage	• Lock doors and ensure only authorised personnel access computers. • Additional security like swipe cards for entry to rooms could be used.

Wide Area Network (WAN)

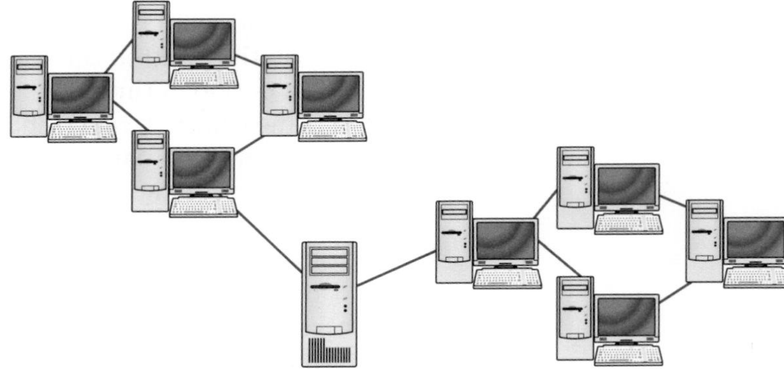

Figure 2.18 A WAN – A network of networks

- A WAN can provide Internet access as well as access to other LANs which can be located anywhere geographically.
- A WAN is a collection of networks connected using a telecommunications link. Most WANs make use of the PSTN.
- The Internet is a WAN.

A **router** is used if LANs are to be connected to the Internet or to a WAN.
A router:

- is device that will translate data from the Internet so that the computers on a LAN can understand it.
- will translate data coming from the LAN to the Internet.
- will find the shortest route to send data across the network.

The main differences between LANs and WANs

LAN	WAN
• Spread over a small geographic area usually one or two buildings.	• Spread over a vast geographic area (countrywide or the world).
• Computers on a LAN can be effectively linked together using copper cabling.	• A network of networks – the most effective way to link networks is using fibre optics or a wireless link (like satellite).

Bandwidth and connection types

- The bandwidth (of a network) is the rate at which data can be transmitted through the communications line in a given period of time.
- It is measured in bits (binary digits) per second.
- The higher the bandwidth, the quicker data will flow along the communications line. This normally means:
  - connection to the Internet is quick so web pages are loaded quickly
  - network traffic is less congested
  - response time on the network is fast so large multimedia files can be down/uploaded quickly.

There are a number of different connection types and each will provide different bandwidths and features. The table below summarises these.

Connection type	Features
PTSN – Public Switched Telephone Network	• Uses the traditional telephone system to allow access to WANs and the Internet. • Low bandwidth 28 kbps (kilobits per second) up to 56 kbps.
ADSL – Asymmetric Digital Subscriber Line	• Provides high bandwidth (known as **broadband**) • It is permanently 'switched on' – there is no need to dial up. • Telephone or fax messages can be received or made while the user is online. • Provides high speed Internet access – up to 8 MB per second.
ISDN – Integrated Services Digital Network	• A home-user ISDN line is a high-speed digital communication line with bandwidth up to 128 kbps. • An ISDN adapter is required to translate data between the computer and the telecommunications line.

Fibre Optic Cable	• Fibres of glass are used to carry signals as pulses of light which can be voice data or computer data. • Very high bandwidth. • They are expensive.
Cable	• Users who subscribe to cable TV (such as NTL) can connect to the Internet using their cable connection.
Satellite	• A computer connects to the Internet and receives and sends data via a satellite dish. • Useful in rural areas where the telephone system is not up to date and where there is no cable TV available. • Satellite connection is expensive. • Users must purchase a satellite dish.
Wireless	• Currently being provided by mobile phone companies using either WAP technology or a device which is plugged into a laptop to enable it to dial up and connect to the Internet. • No cables are required. • Expensive to use.

Communications protocol

A communications protocol is an agreed standard for sending or receiving data on a computer network.
Facts about protocols:

- The Internet protocol is Transmission Control Protocol / Internet Protocol (TCP/IP).
- A router allows networks using different protocols to communicate.
- Protocols are needed to make sure that data is not lost and that computers can send and receive data successfully.

Connecting to and using the Internet

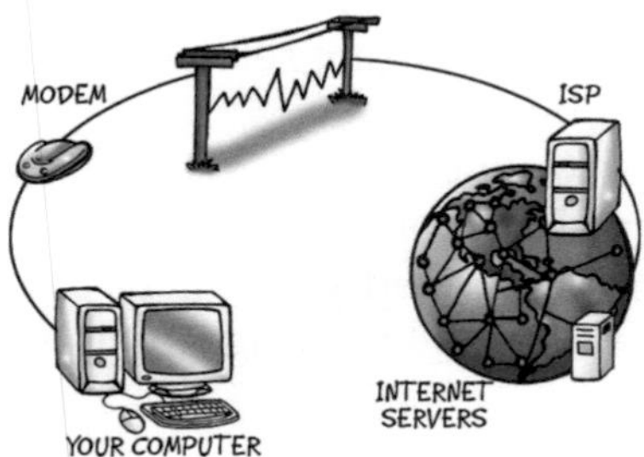

Figure 2.19 Connecting to the Internet

A single user needs a computer and:

	Type	Purpose	Example
Telecommunications line	Hardware	• Provides the cabling and pathways on which data can travel to and from the Internet.	Dial up, ISDN, ADSL
Modem (MOdulator-DEModulator)	Hardware	• A modem converts the signals from your computer so that they can travel along the telecommunications line to your ISP. • A dial-up modem (which is usually internal to your computer) converts analogue signals from the telephone line to digital signals that your computer can work with.	Dial-up modem/ADSL modem/ISDN adapter/Cable modem/Router containing ADSL modem (e.g. ADSL wireless router)
Internet Service Provider	Company	• Provides a connection to the Internet and a range of services (see list below).	AOL, BT, Virgin etc.
ISP software	Software	• Dial up using the ISP software.	CD-ROM supplied by your ISP. Should be installed on your computer. Contains drivers for the modem and dial-up software.
Browser software	Software	To view web pages (see the features of a browser below).	Internet Explorer, Mozilla Firefox etc.

Internet Service Provider (ISP)

Sells Internet access to companies or individuals and provides some of the following:

- A variety of bandwidth options.
- An e-mail service with virus protection, which allows users to send and receive e-mail.
- Web-hosting service which allows users to upload their own web pages.
- Online and telephone assistance.
- Junk mail blocker.
- Pop-up advertisement blocker.
- Website filtering (to filter out unsuitable content).

Browser software

Web pages are usually designed in HTML (HyperText Mark-up Language) format. Browsers are programmed to interpret the HTML in order to display the contents on screen.
The features on a browser toolbar include:

- An address bar – allows the user to enter the web address or URL of the website they wish to visit.
- A navigation bar – allows the user to navigate between the web pages visited.
- A bookmark or favourites option – allows the user to keep a list of favourite website URLs. The user can also set the home page.
- A search engine – most browsers provide software/a program or a website which helps a user find information on the Web. Google is an example of a search engine.
- A history button – the browser will usually keep a list of web pages visited in a previous user-defined number of days and weeks.
- Filtering options – allows content to be filtered. The user can:
  - filter content and language
  - block websites which may not be viewed.

Understanding the URL

The URL is the **Uniform Resource Locator** – it is the website address. For example the URL for the CCEA website is http://www.ccea.org.uk.

http://	HyperText Transfer Protocol – the protocol used to exchange data. (**ftp://** – file transfer protocol – is another protocol. It allows users to upload web pages to web servers.)
www.ccea.org	The **domain name** which includes the name of the host server. **ccea.org** is the **Second level** domain name and it must be unique on the Internet. On its own **.org** is the **Top level** domain name and it indicates the purpose of the organisation.
uk	The **country level** domain name – in this case United Kingdom.

A URL can be extended to direct the browser to a particular page or file on a website, for example the URL **http://www.ccea.org.uk/gcseict/questions.html** would display a page called **questions.html** contained within a folder called **gcseict**.

The Internet and the World Wide Web (WWW)

The Internet and the World Wide Web are two separate things although each requires the other.

Internet	World Wide Web
• A network of networks – it is a means of connecting computers. • It does not contain information itself but provides transport links for data to pass between computers.	• An application which runs on the Internet and is the largest and most used service on the Internet.
	Pages on the WWW: • are written using the programming language HTML • are usually viewed using a browser • contain **hypertext** which provides the user with clickable links to other pages on the Web • can contain sound, video, animation, graphics and hypertext as well as simple text.

Intranets

Facts:

- An intranet is a website on a network within an organisation.
- Only authorised users can log on and use an intranet.
- Pages on an intranet are generally viewed using a browser.

Advantages:

- Used to share information, to communicate and to aid discussion by means of bulletin boards and messaging facilities.
- Less paper produced by an organisation.
- Employees can access information at any time.
- Improves an organisation's internal communication.

Some schools have an intranet which is used to communicate with both staff and pupils.
Teachers can use an intranet to:

- visit departmental websites which contain notes about topics being studied and homework, and provide feedback on tests
- communicate using the e-mail facility with pupils and other staff within the school
- share exemplary pupil work with the school community
- share resources with other subject teachers

- book resources or rooms through a central booking system.

Pupils can use an intranet to:

- access notes and materials to work independently
- communicate digitally with teachers about problems or difficulties with homework
- e-mail or upload homework to teachers
- find out about general school information.

Communications technology

E-mail

E-mail (electronic mail) is a service provided on the Internet. It allows users to send messages from a computer across the Internet at anytime.
To send an e-mail you need an e-mail address, for example:

E-mail allows a user to:

- create a message
- reply to a message
- forward a message to other users
- send a message to a list of people
- send files as attachments
- save and print a message.

The sender has available the following boxes:

To...	The sender of the e-mail enters the e-mail addresses of the recipients here.
Cc...	Carbon Copy: The sender enters the e-mail address of people receiving a copy of the e-mail for information purposes only.
Bcc...	Blind Carbon Copy: The sender enters the e-mail address of people receiving a blind copy of the e-mail. Their addresses will not be seen by the main recipients of the message.
Subject	The sender types a short description of what the e-mail is about.
Attachments	The sender can attach files of almost any format to the e-mail.

Advantages of e-mail

- Flexible – can be sent or received anytime day or night.
- Easily managed – no paper is used and all e-mails arrive in the inbox.
- Fast – delivered almost instantly to any location in the world.
- Inexpensive – compared with telephone calls, faxes and courier services.
- Filtering of e-mail can be done easily – protecting users from inappropriate communication.
- Attachments – the sender can attach files to an e-mail, so sound, graphics and text files can be easily distributed.
- Secure and private – emails can be sent securely and privately unlike faxes and telephone calls.

Disadvantages of e-mail

- Technology – the sender and recipient must have access to the Internet.
- It is easy to insert a wrong address into the **To...** box. A confidential e-mail could be sent to the wrong person.
- Spam – unwanted e-mails, perhaps selling or advertising products, can be received. This is like electronic junk mail.
- Users are not notified of new e-mails unless they are logged on to the e-mail system.

Facsimile

Facts:

- Facsimile machines, or fax machines, work by making a digital copy of an image which is fed into the machine. This image is then transmitted to another fax machine via a telephone line. The receiving fax then prints an image based on reconstructing the signals coming in via the telephone line.
- A fax machine is made up of a printer and an optical scanner.
- Modern fax machines can scan, print and copy documents as well as perform their fax function.

Advantages of faxes

- Can be used to transmit drawings, and handwritten or signed documents.
- Do not transfer viruses and are less likely to be the subject of hacking.
- Can be used to send documents to recipients who do not have an e-mail address.

Disadvantages of faxes

- Must be connected to a telephone line.
- Usually operate in black and white.
- Can be expensive – running costs include toner cartridges for printing, electrical charges and the cost of telephone calls every time a fax is sent.

- The receiving fax machine must be free to receive the document otherwise it will have to be sent again.

Video conferencing

Video conferencing uses the Internet to transmit pictures and sound between computers.
The following equipment is needed:

- A video camera or webcam to capture pictures.
- Microphone and sound system to receive sound.
- A screen to view other participants.
- A high bandwidth telecommunications line.
- Videoconferencing software.

Advantages:

- Allows collaboration with team members without them having to leave their desks. Team members can be within a company or within other companies anywhere in the world.
- Visual contact means more realistic meetings than with phone conferencing (audio only).
- Full multimedia presentations can be made using the application sharing tool.
- Meetings can be set up on demand by connecting up to the videolink.
- No travel costs for the company.
- No travel time for the employee.

Instant messaging

Instant messaging allows users to use text to communicate instantly with each other. When a user types a message all of the users logged in can see the message instantly.

Bulletin boards

Bulletin boards provide text-based messaging but it is not instant or interactive. A user will log on to a bulletin board and 'post' a message. It may be a few hours or days before a reply is posted on the bulletin board.

Mobile phones and Portable Digital Assistants (PDAs)

Figure 2.20 Mobile phone

- Communication can be via a telephone call or by using SMS (Short Message Service – users can send text messages instantly to other SMS-enabled phones on any network. The text message can get through even when a call is in progress).
- Mobile phones now have many features such as a camera, MP3 player, voice recognition, diary etc.
- Mobile phone technology means that phones can 'roam' (pick up another network and be used in any country in the world where there is network coverage).
- Voicemail enables callers to leave a message if the owner of the telephone is not available.

- WAP phones can be used to browse the Internet, for example workers who are out of the office can:
  - view train timetables
  - view traffic information
  - check weather conditions
  - send and receive emails.

PDAs are also WAP-enabled. (WAP is Wireless Applications Protocol and was designed to allow hand-held devices access to the Internet.)

Digital image systems

Digital television

Facts:

- Conventional television was transmitted using analogue signals.
- Digital signals are used to transmit digital TV channels.
- The digital signal has to be decoded so that a normal TV can show the images and sounds.

Disadvantages

- A digital receiver is needed to convert digital signals into analogue signals for display on a TV.
- Not all digital TV is free – subscriptions can be expensive.

Advantages

- Signals can be compressed, therefore the amount of data which can be sent on a digital signal is much greater.
- Can be interactive because the communications lines can transmit and receive data.
- Is less affected by interference than analogue television.
- Provides a sharper, clearer picture and better quality sound.
- Pictures are broadcast in widescreen format.
- More channels are available on digital TV.
- Viewers can view programmes from different camera angles.

Digital cameras

Facts:

The images taken using a digital camera are stored on magnetic, optical or flash media. Examples of these are smart cards or memory sticks which can be directly inserted in a PC.

Digital and conventional cameras compared

Digital	Conventional
• Often expensive to buy. • Photos taken can be downloaded to a PC and edited or manipulated using a graphics package. • Not all photos need to be printed – the user can delete unwanted photos from memory. • No expensive developing costs – images can be printed at home. • No waiting to see photos – they can be viewed on the LCD screen immediately. • The quality of photos can vary according to the output device producing them. • Photos are provided in JPEG format and can be e-mailed or placed in other documents.	• Relatively cheap to buy. • Only hardcopies of photographs are produced. • All photos in the film have to be printed – this can be wasteful and expensive if the photos are not of good quality. • The film from the camera has to be taken to a specialist so it can be developed and the photos printed – this is expensive. • The photographer has to wait until photos are developed before viewing them. • Photos are of a very high quality. • Hardcopy of photos have to be scanned if they are to be used in digital documents.

- Resolution refers to the number of pixels which make up the image.
- The more pixels the higher the resolution and the sharper the image.
- Pictures taken at high resolution take up more storage space than those taken at a lower resolution.

Revision questions

LANs and WANs

1 Expand the following acronyms/abbreviations:

a LAN　b WAN　c WWW　d ISP
e HTML　f URL　g ISDN　h PSTN
i ADSL　j PC

2 A school makes use of a LAN.

a What is a LAN?
b Draw a diagram of how a LAN might be organised.
c What is the role of **switches** in a LAN?

3 a Within a network there is a communications protocol. Explain this term.
b What is a WAN?
c What infrastructure is needed to support a WAN?
d How could organisations make use of a WAN?

4 a List **three** connection types which can be used when connecting to the Internet.
b Which connection type could a company use to ensure that they make greatest use of the communications highways available to them. Give two reasons for your answer.

5 A Local Area Network (LAN) is a combination of cables, computers and file servers.

a State **two** advantages of having computers connected on a LAN.
b State **two** disadvantages of having computers connected on a LAN.

6 A user is to be connected to the WWW.

a What is the WWW?
b What hardware is required to do this?
c What software is required to make the Internet connection?
d List **four** services provided by an ISP.
e What does the term **bandwidth** mean with regards to an Internet connection?
f How does bandwidth influence the download speed of data?
g Give **two** examples of search engines you have used on the Internet.
h What features of a web browser help a user ensure that inappropriate content is not accessed.
i List **three** other features provided by a typical web browser.

7 a Draw a diagram of a network system. It should show:
- the PCs
- the links between the PCs and the switch
- the links between the switch and server
- the file server
- the router.

b Give the function of each of the above.

8 What bandwidths are offered by the following?

a PSTN
b ISDN
c ADSL
d optical fibre

9 http://www.google.co.uk/sample/weather.htm is a URL. What does each part of the URL tell us?

Network security

10 Describe how a network is protected by:

a passwords
b access levels (tiered access)
c encryption.

11 Backup of data is very important.

a What is a backup?
b How should data on a network be backed up?
c How should data on a single-user PC be backed up?

Internet communication systems

12 List the main differences between a conventional camera and a digital camera.

13 List **three** ways in which a person can communicate using a mobile phone.

14 How can a portable device, such as a mobile phone or PDA, help travelling salespersons do their job?

15 A school in Northern Ireland wishes to make links with a school in the USA. List and describe the communication technology which could be used to make the links.

Examination questions

1 Aaron asked his parents to buy a digital TV package.

a What is the difference between digital TV and analogue TV? [2]

b List **two** advantages to Aaron of having digital TV. [2]

c List **one** advantage to Aaron of having analogue TV. [1]

CCEA 2006

2 The school office of Great Days College uses technology to communicate with parents, governors and suppliers of equipment. This is done mainly through the fax machine, telephone and letters.

a E-mail has been made available to office staff and the Principal wants to get rid of the fax machine.

i Give **two** situations when using a fax machine is better than using e-mail. [2]

ii How could the secretary send letters to many people quickly by using e-mail? [2]

b The Principal decides to make a link with a school in Russia. Videoconferencing will be required.

i What is videoconferencing? [2]

ii Name **three** pieces of hardware required for videoconferencing. [3]

iii How could the project be made more successful through the use of videoconferencing? [1]

CCEA 2006

3 Brenda's Bakery is expanding to include shops all over Northern Ireland. Brenda wants to link all her stores using the Internet.

a Explain the following Internet-related terms to Brenda.

i bandwidth
ii optical fibre
iii ADSL [6]

Brenda would like to be able to use videoconferencing but cannot decide if she should use the PSTN or broadband.

b Say which you would recommend and give **two** reasons for your answer. [3]

c **i** List **two** items of hardware Brenda will need to connect to the Internet. [2]

ii Name **one** item of software Brenda will need to connect to the Internet. [1]

d Why are protocols important in network communication? [2]

CCEA 2007

4 A local school is expanding its Local Area Network (LAN) to include a wireless connection.

a Give **one** advantage to the pupils of being able to access the network using wireless connection. [1]

b Apart from security give **one** disadvantage to the school of using a wireless connection. [1]

c Why does the school need a router? [1]

d List **two** tasks carried out by the operating system on a network. [2]

e What type of storage media should the school use to backup their server? [1]

f How often should they back up their server? [1]

g The school want to make their intranet and the Internet available to pupils. Give **two** differences between the Internet and the intranet. [2]

CCEA 2007

5 Kate has a PC at home. She wants to connect to the Internet. She needs the following:

- an ISP
- ISP software
- browser software
- a telecommunications line
- a modem.

a Expand the abbreviation **ISP**. [1]

b Why does she need the browser software? [1]

c What does a modem do when a user is connected to the Internet?

[1]

d Kate chooses an ISP. List **three** services which ISPs commonly provide.

[3]

Kate's parents decide to filter her Internet access.

e **i** How will filtering affect Kate when she is using the Internet?

[1]

ii Give **one** reason why Kate's parents want to filter her Internet access?

[1]

Kate visits a TV and radio company's website to get information for her Home Economics project. The website broadcasts radio and TV programmes and allows the public to post messages about healthy living.

f **i** Give **one** advantage to the company of the public being able to listen to programmes live on the Internet.

[1]

ii Give **one** disadvantage of allowing the public to leave comments about the company on the message board.

[1]

CCEA 2007

C2(d) Applications of ICT

In this section you will see how all of the components you have learned about work together. Computer systems and communication technology are used in almost every aspect of our daily lives. You will see how the hardware, software and communication links are used by different organisations for different purposes. At the end of this section you should understand the advantages of using ICT.

Acronyms and abbreviations

Acronym/abbreviation	Meaning
EFT	Electronic Funds Transfer
POS	Point Of Sale
EPOS	Electronic Point Of Sale
EFTPOS	Electronic Funds Transfer Point Of Sale
ATM	Automatic Teller Machine
PIN	Personal Identification Number
ADC	Analogue to Digital Converter

You must know about the following applications of ICT:

- Electronic monetary processing
- Batch processing in billing systems
- Virtual reality in training and entertainment
- Computers in control, including greenhouses, traffic control and domestic control systems
- Online services, including shopping, banking, reservations and e-commerce

Electronic monetary processing

Many customers pay for goods in shops and online using credit or debit cards. Money is transferred electronically from the customer's account to the retailer's account using specialised secure equipment. No cash changes hands. This is called Electronic Funds Transfer (EFT).

EFT in shops

Shops use computer technology as follows:

- Point of Sale (POS) – an ordinary supermarket checkout till.
- Electronic Point Of Sale (EPOS) – a supermarket checkout till with a barcode reader which is connected to a computer.
- Electronic Funds Transfer Point of Sale (EFTPOS) – a supermarket checkout till with a barcode reader which is connected to a computer and which can transfer money from a customer's account using a credit or debit card.

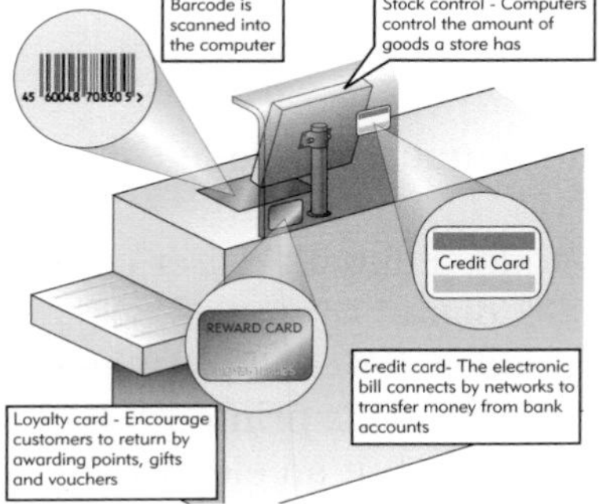

Figure 2.21 Control at the shop checkout

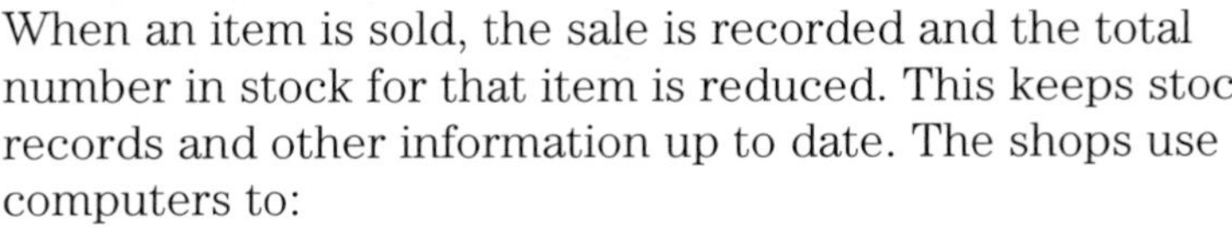

The EFTPOS is connected to the shop's central computer. When an item is sold, the sale is recorded and the total number in stock for that item is reduced. This keeps stock records and other information up to date. The shops use computers to:

- assist in stock control
- order new stock
- calculate profit margins
- assist managers in decision-making.

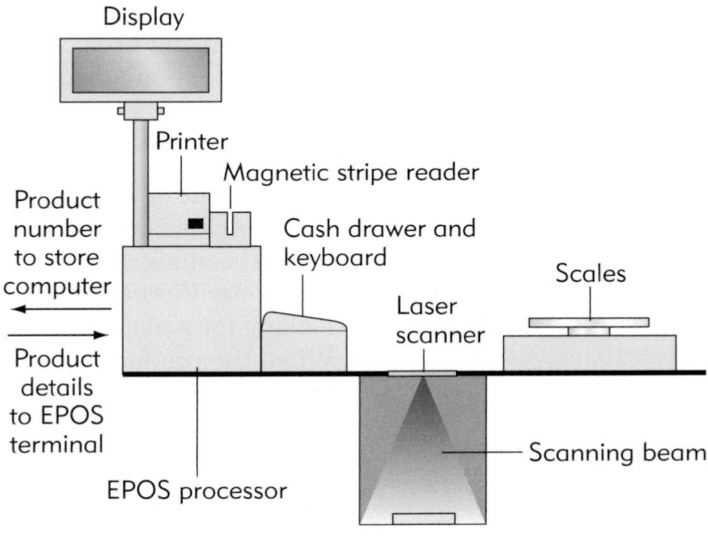

Figure 2.22 EFTPOS

Components of an EFTPOS

Barcodes

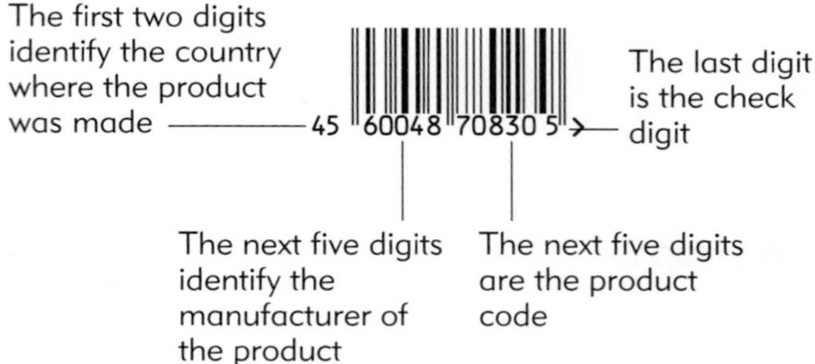

Figure 2.23 Barcode

- A manufacturer includes a barcode on an item's packaging.
- Each product normally contains a unique barcode consisting of 13 digits.
- A barcode contains a product code, a manufacturer code, the country of origin and a check digit.
- Shops can attach their own barcodes, for example when buying from the meat counter a barcode is printed.
- Barcodes cannot be read by a human, but an electronic reader gives a high accuracy rate.
- Apart from their use in shops, barcodes are also used to:
  - track parcels in the post office or courier service
  - track luggage at airports
  - issue books in libraries.

Barcode readers

A barcode reader uses laser beam light to read and enter the code details automatically.
Each time a barcode is scanned at an EPOS terminal the following activities occur:

- The barcode scanner reads the barcode on the product.
- The barcode is sent to the branch's computer (which holds the stock database) by the EFTPOS terminal.
- The computer uses the barcode to search the stock file looking for a matching product.
- When the product is found, the product price and product description are sent back to the EFTPOS terminal.
- The branch's computer updates the stock level for the product to show that one (or more) has been sold.
- The good's price and description are displayed at the EFTPOS terminal and printed on a receipt.
- If a barcode is damaged it cannot be read but the numbers it represents can still be keyed in.

Electronic Funds Transfer System

The customer uses a credit card or a debit card, which contains a magnetic stripe and/or a chip.
The EFTPOS terminal contains a magnetic stripe reader, or chip and PIN system, which is used to carry out the transaction.

1. **Card swiped/inserted in Chip and Pin terminal:** The customer details are entered from the stripe or chip on the card and the amount of the transaction is also entered.
2. **PIN (Personal Identification Number) entered:** The customer enters their PIN to verify the transaction. (In some older systems, customers do not use a PIN, but are asked to sign the receipt to confirm the transaction.)
3. **Authorisation check:** Approval for the transaction is requested.
4. **Receipt printed:** If the transaction is approved by the bank or credit card company, two copies of a receipt of the transaction are printed – one for the customer and one for the shop.

Advantages of EFT

To the customer	To the vendor
• Credit card slips automatically printed at the checkout. • Debit cards can be used to obtain cash at the checkout. • The money involved in the transaction is debited from your account immediately so the balance displayed in your account is always up to date. • Some customers feel more secure if they don't have to carry large amounts of cash in their wallet/purse. • Credit or debit cards can be used in any country – local currency is not needed for purchases.	• Payment to the shop's bank account is guaranteed as long as the transactions are properly authorised. • Less administration/paperwork with EFT so less staff required. • Reduced concerns about forgery. • The shop collects less cash so there is less chance of theft. • If the money is deposited immediately in the shop's bank account it may receive more interest.

Automatic Teller Machines (ATMs)

ATMs allow a customer to gain access to their account 24 hours a day, 7 days a week.
They offer a range of services, such as:

- cash withdrawal (with or without a receipt)
- ordering a bank statement

- ordering a new cheque book
- getting a current account balance
- printing a mini-statement (usually the most recent transactions)
- informing customers of new banking services
- buying mobile phone call credit
- changing a PIN.

A bank's ATM can be used by customers of other banks but in general they are limited to cash withdrawal with or without a receipt.

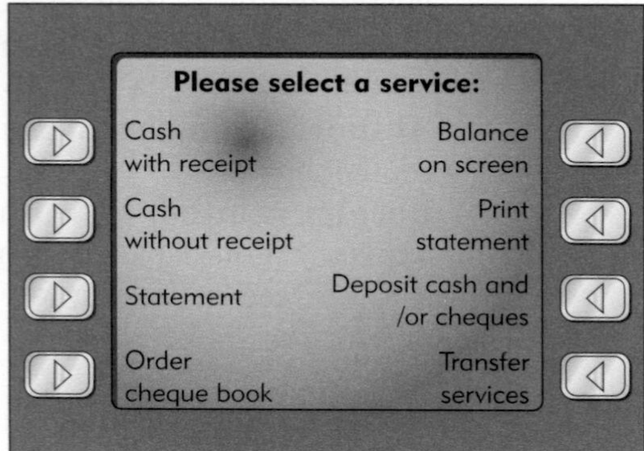

Figure 2.24 ATM screen

ATM operation

To use an ATM the person needs a bank credit/debit card normally containing a magnetic stripe or chip. The magnetic stripe stores information about the customer.

1 The customer inserts bank credit/debit card in the ATM.
2 The ATM requests the card's PIN.
3 The customer enters the PIN.
4 The PIN entered is checked against the PIN stored for the customer's account. (This is a security check designed to protect customer details against unauthorised access.)
5 If the PIN is correct the ATM allows the customer access to all the services. If the PIN is incorrect the customer will be asked to re-enter it. (The customer will be given only a limited number of attempts to enter the correct PIN (usually three).)
6 If the customer wants to withdraw cash a check is done to ensure that they have enough money in the account.
7 The customer's account will be updated with the details of the transaction.

There are many advantages for both the customer and the bank of using ATMs, such as:

- It saves money because banks need fewer employees behind counters, as there are fewer customers in the bank.
- Customers have access, 24 hours a day and 7 days a week to their accounts.
- The system makes it impossible for a customer to withdraw cash from their account unless they have sufficient funds.
- There is no need for customers to carry large amounts of cash, as ATMs are widely available – this reduces theft.
- Using a PIN number is more secure than using a signature on a cheque to obtain cash.
- People can use ATMs that don't belong to their bank – this provides access to funds all over the world.

Magnetic stripe and smart cards

Figure 2.25 Credit card and microchip

Magnetic stripe

Magnetic stripes are used on most cash and credit cards. They are also used on:

- customer loyalty cards to collect rewards for shopping
- membership cards for clubs and societies to store membership details
- 'keys' for hotel rooms (instead of a traditional room key).

A magnetic stripe reader is an integral part of an EFTPOS terminal and an ATM.

Advantages	Disadvantages
• Data can be read from the stripe or written to the stripe. • Magnetic stripe technology is relatively cheap.	• The magnetic stripe is designed to store only a small amount of data. • Although the details held on a magnetic stripe cannot be read directly by a person, they can be forged. Thus the person who owns the card normally has to sign to verify the details. • Data on the magnetic stripe can be corrupted if it is exposed to a magnetic field.

Smart cards

The smart card was designed to replace the magnetic stripe. Although the plastic card is similar in size it contains a tiny embedded microchip. It is sometimes called an integrated chip card (ICC).
New credit/cash cards contain both a stripe and a chip. At present their main uses are for:

- mobile phones (SIM card)
- satellite TV receivers (for example Sky TV cards)
- pre-pay phone cards
- retail loyalty schemes
- personal identification
- access to buildings.

Contactless smart cards are used to pay motorway tolls in the USA. The technology at the toll booth allows a motorist using an appropriate card to pass through without stopping. The amount due is deducted from the card automatically without physical contact between the card reader and the card.

Advantages	Disadvantages
• The microchip can store more data than a typical magnetic stripe. • Highly flexible technology which means they can be used in many applications. • Almost completely unaffected by magnetic field. • More secure than magnetic stripe technology.	• Failure rate of chips is high. • Discarded cards (e.g. phone cards) can be reprogrammed and used as counterfeit cards.

Billing applications

- Bills are a request for payment, such as for a utility like electricity, gas or telephone.
- Bills are sent on a monthly or quarterly basis.
- Producing utility bills for everyone in the country at the same time requires a large computer system and is called batch processing.

Batch processing

Batch processing involves collecting groups (or batches) of similar data over a period of time and inputting it to a computer system. These batches of data are then processed collectively without human intervention or involvement. Due to the huge amount of data it normally takes a long time for the computer to process the data.

Applications which make use of batch processing include:

- utility billing systems
- payroll system of a large organisation.

Consider the production of electricity bills. The main files are:

- **master file** – stores information which does not change between bills, such as customer account number, customer name, address details, last meter reading, amount of electricity used over the past number of quarters.
- **transaction file** – a temporary file containing the customer account number and the current meter reading. This information will be used to update the master file.

Note that the transaction file is sorted into the same order as the customer file before updating. This makes updating the master file much quicker as less searching for records has to be done.

Stages in producing an electricity bill

1 Meters are read by the meter reader and recorded on the customer data collection form.
2 Customer meter readings are placed together as batches.
3 These are entered into the computer system.
4 The data is checked, using data verification and data validation techniques.
5 At this stage any errors are notified, such as the wrong number of digits in the customer account number, and an error report is produced.
6 The validated data is used to create a transaction file.
7 The transaction file is sorted into the same order as the master file using the key field, which is normally the customer account number.
8 The sorted transaction file is stored and will be used to easily allow matching transaction records with master file records.
9 Both the master file and the transaction file are used to calculate and print the customer bills.
10 The details on the transaction file are used to update the master file and this is saved as a new master file.
11 Customers are sent their bill.
12 The new master file will be used to calculate the bill in the next quarter and the process continues.

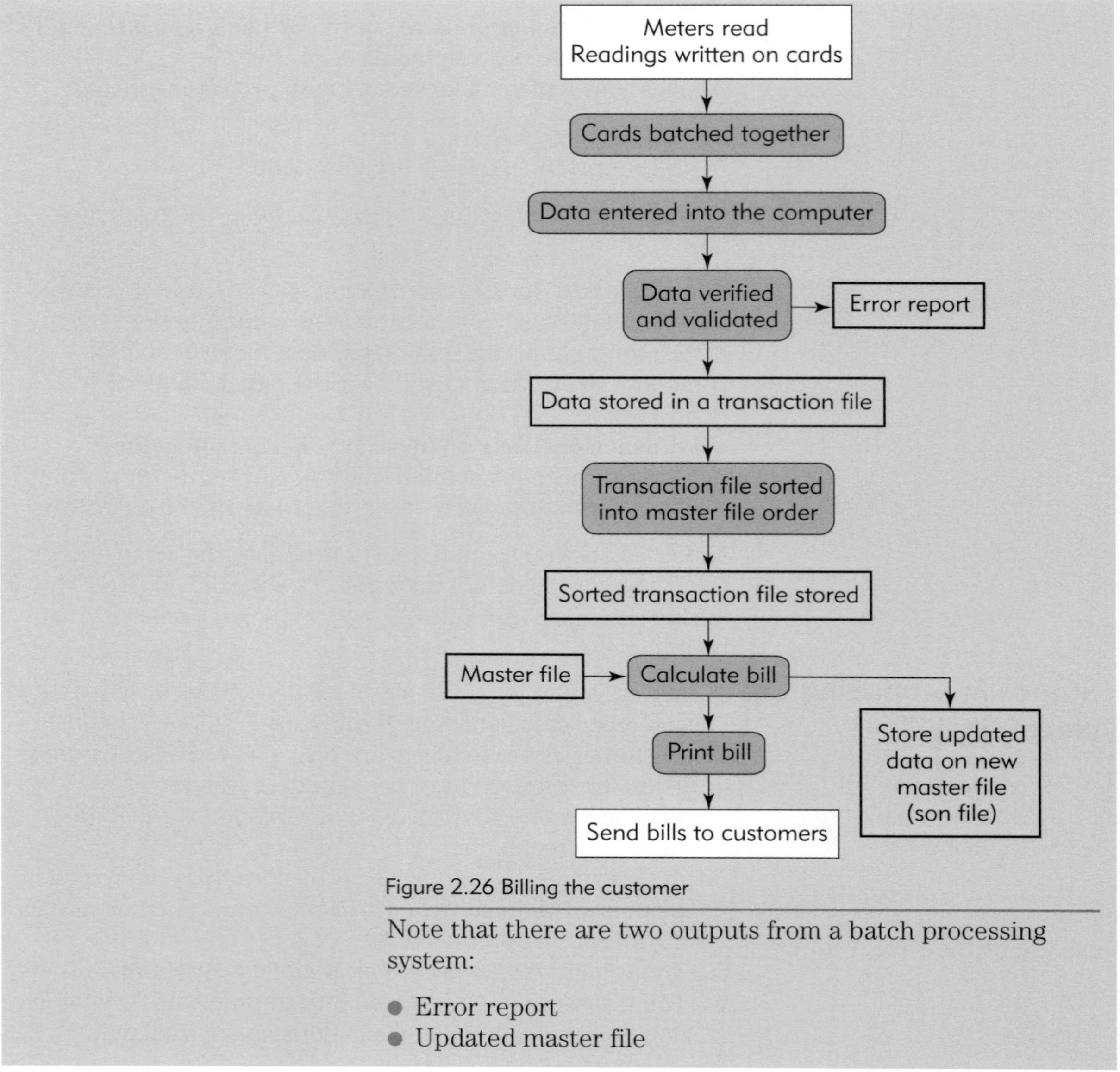

Figure 2.26 Billing the customer

Note that there are two outputs from a batch processing system:

- Error report
- Updated master file

Virtual reality in training and entertainment applications

Simulation and virtual reality

A simulation involves putting values into a model to see how it behaves in different environments. This could mean testing cars to see what happens when they crash, creating strong winds or even an earthquake to see how a shopping centre would react in the conditions. This process helps the designers to trial ideas before the real product is developed.

Key term	Meaning
Computer model	A program with a set of rules which describes the behaviour of an object or a process.
Computer simulation	A program which models a real-life situation.
Virtual reality system	A system that enables a person to move through and react within an environment simulated by a computer. Users usually wear stereoscopic helmets (HMD – Head Mounted Devices) to allow 3-D visual hearing, hand gloves for touch sensations to control the model and tracking devices or joysticks to navigate around the environment.

Examples of applications that use virtual reality include building designs, airlines, medicine, computer games.

Building designs

A new building, such as a house, can be designed on a computer using virtual reality. The house is created using powerful modelling programs.
Advantages:

- Before the house is built the computer can be used for a walkthrough using a stereoscopic helmet.
- The house can also be viewed by different users from a range of different heights and angles.
- Old buildings built thousands of years ago, that no longer exist, can be recreated using virtual reality so we can learn more about our past.

Airlines

Aircraft simulators and virtual reality are used to train pilots. The simulator does not look like an aeroplane – it is a full-size replica of a typical cockpit that never leaves the ground.
Advantages

- safe – if the pilot makes a mistake a crash is simulated but does not result in loss of life.
- cheap
  - if the pilot makes a mistake, there is no cost
  - training using a real aeroplane is expensive in terms of fuel costs and loss of possible airfares by taking a plane out of service.
- real
  - it gives the pilot an experience of a range of real environments – extreme conditions like bad weather or landing conditions can be simulated

- all the pilot's actions are recorded by the computer system and used to provide feedback to the pilot and trainers.

Medicine

Scanners can collect large amounts of data about a person's internal system and biological make up. A computer can then produce a 3-D model of the whole or part of the body, creating a virtual patient.
Virtual reality is used in the following areas of medicine:

- diagnosis of illness – by examining the detailed accurate images produced by the 3-D model, quick and accurate diagnosis can be made.
- planning, education and training – surgeons can plan and practise (simulate) a particular operation on a 'virtual patient' before actually carrying it out on a real patient. They can predict the outcome of the operation using this technique. They can repeat an operation on a 'virtual patient' and improve their skills thereby minimising risk to people.

In addition to simulation and virtual reality, computers can help surgeons by allowing global consultations, whereby they can consult with other specialists around the world by using technology such as video conferencing.

Gaming

Many computer games are designed with virtual reality features. Users are given the feeling of being a part of the game, rather than just playing the game.
The user can sometimes wear an HMD and gloves to play the game. In other games the user sits on a racing car, or on a device like it, and watches the computer screen. The game works by responding to inputs from the user devices including the throttle, the gears and the steering wheel. The user is given the impression of driving a real car, including the visual, sound effects and the sensation of acceleration. More games that use virtual reality are appearing in amusement arcades.
Advantages of simulation:

- Dangerous activites can be simulated without danger to individuals.
- Users can practise activities like snowboarding without going to the slopes.

Computers in control

Key term	Meaning
Sensor	An input device, which can be used to measure almost any physical quantity. For example temperature sensors measure heat intensity.
Real-time processing	The computer receives a message or input and responds (almost) immediately. This is important in control systems that ensure the correct action is taken in time to prevent damage or accident.
Data logging	The automatic capture and storage of data without human intervention.
Data logging interval	The time which passes between recording each reading.
Analogue to digital conversion	Sensors record data in analogue format. This data must be converted to digital format so that the computer can work with it. This is done by an analogue to digital converter (ADC).
Feedback	When the output of a system is compared with its input to affect its performance. ● input: data is recorded. ● processing: a comparison of the data and the range of values allowed is carried out. ● output: if the data is outside the range of values allowed the system will activate a device to correct this.

Examples of feedback

A home heating system uses a temperature sensor to monitor the room temperature at regular intervals.

- The data is fed into the computer.
- When the computer processes the data one of two possible outputs will occur, either to turn the heating on or turn the heating off.
- The result will be a change in temperature.
- When the temperature is read next it will be higher/lower. This means that the output from the system (switching the heating on or off) has affected the input (the temperature has changed).

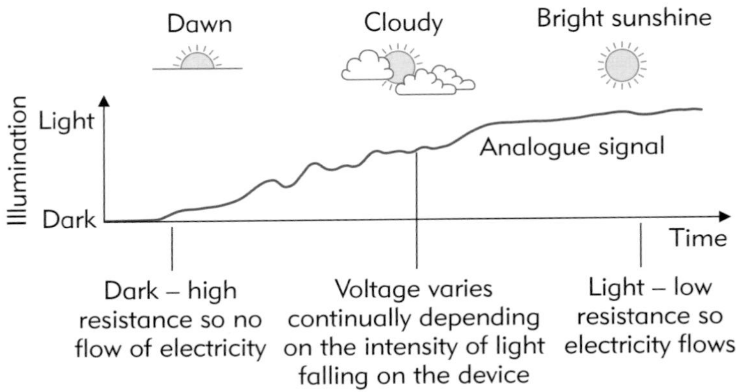

Figure 2.27 Digitising real-world measurements

The use of computers to log data:

- is more accurate than human-collected data
- in some cases is safer than with a human collecting data
- means data can be stored over a period of time and then analysed by special/dedicated software.

You must know about the following systems:

Greenhouse control systems Computers are used in greenhouses. Sensors measure temperature, light, humidity and dampness in soil.	The computer has a set of values for each factor which is being measured. If the factor goes outside the range of values something will happen in the greenhouse to correct this. **Temperature:** Input – temperature sensor measures temperature. Comparison (or processing) – temperature is checked against the allowable range. Action (or output) – the computer sends a 'too hot' message to switch on fans, open windows or switch off heaters. – the computer sends a 'too cold' message to switch on heaters etc., again turning off the heaters when the temperature rises to an acceptable level. Result: temperature readings will be within the range allowed. **Light** Input – a light sensor measures light level Comparison (or processing) – light level is checked against allowable range. Action (or output) – when the amount of natural light falls the computer may turn on the lights in the greenhouse and when the amount of natural light increases the computer may turn off the lights in the greenhouse Result – light level readings will be within the range allowed. **Humidity** Input – a humidity sensor will measure how much water vapour is in the air. Comparison (or processing) – humidity is checked against allowable range. Action (or output) – the computer sends a message to turn on or off the water sprinklers. Result: humidity readings will be within the range allowed. (Similar process could apply to the soil sensors.)
Traffic control systems These systems are used in cities to keep traffic moving. Computers are used to control traffic lights, car park management and vehicle speeding.	**Traffic lights** Most control of traffic lights in cities is centralised. They are programmed to vary in operation throughout a day. For example they may remain green for longer during busy periods on priority roads to avoid traffic build up. These systems are often called vehicle actuation systems. Input – traffic sensors detect and count the cars over a period of time and send the data back to the main computer. Comparison (or processing) – is traffic passing at the allowable rate? Action (or output) – signals are sent back to the lights to change the timings of the light sequence. If the number of cars passing is too high the computer may send a signal to keep lights green for longer, so that more cars will pass in a period of time. It is possible to ensure that traffic lights are all green along the route of an emergency vehicle. Result: the readings measuring the number of cars passing will be within the range allowed. Each set of lights can also react automatically to local events such as people wishing to cross roads. By pressing a button, the local control box will allow the lights to be changed to red for a short period of time.

Car park management

Computer-controlled systems can direct cars around a city to car parks with available space. Sensors are used to automatically log each car on entry and exit.

Input – the system calculates the number of vehicles entering and leaving a car park at regular time intervals.

Comparison (or processing) – is the number of cars in the car park less than the total number of spaces available?

Action (or output) – if the number of cars in the car park is less than the total number of spaces available the system will display the number of free spaces on large electronic displays.

Speed control

Police forces make use of computer technology to sense and record the speeds of individual cars.

Input – sensors detect car speeds.

Comparison (or processing) – if the speed of the car is greater than the speed limit a camera will automatically take a photograph of the car and record its registration number, speed, location and the time and date of the incident. All these details can be printed on the photograph.

Action (or output) – the owner is sent a fine and notice of penalty points awarded. The data logged by each camera is analysed to produce data about roads where speeding is a problem.

Special sensors built into traffic lights can also detect cars driving through red lights.

Domestic control systems

These are used to control devices in the home by using a microprocessor, which is inside the device (an embedded computer).

Control devices are found in many domestic appliances, such as washing machines, heating controllers, burglar alarms, DVD players and microwaves.

The embedded computer in each device will control the input and output devices attached to the device.

Consider a typical automatic washing machine:

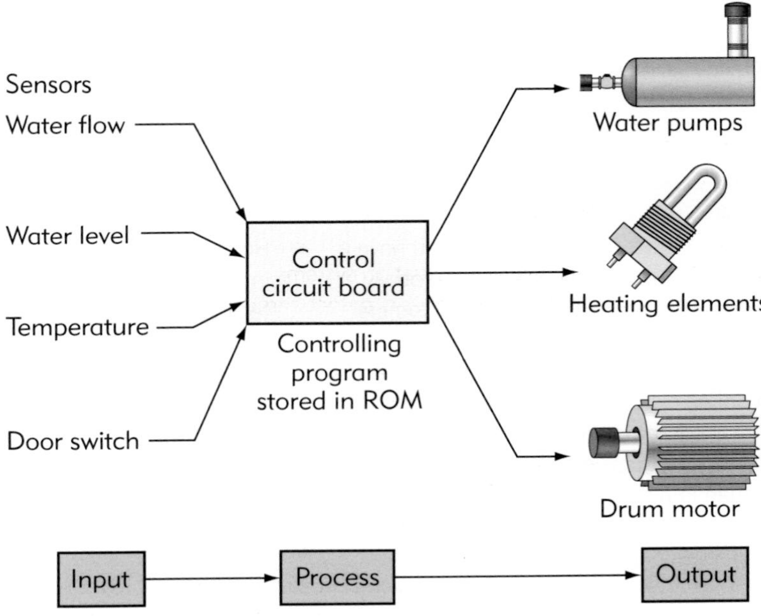

Figure 2.28 Components of a typical washing machine

The user selects a washing cycle. The microprocessor carries out a stored sequence of instructions, such as:

- turning on and off switches for water intake and water outlet
- turning on and off switches for the water heater to heat the water to a given temperature
- controlling the water pump and controlling the drum speed.

Sensors used include:

- water flow sensors
- temperature sensors
- door open/close sensors.

Online services

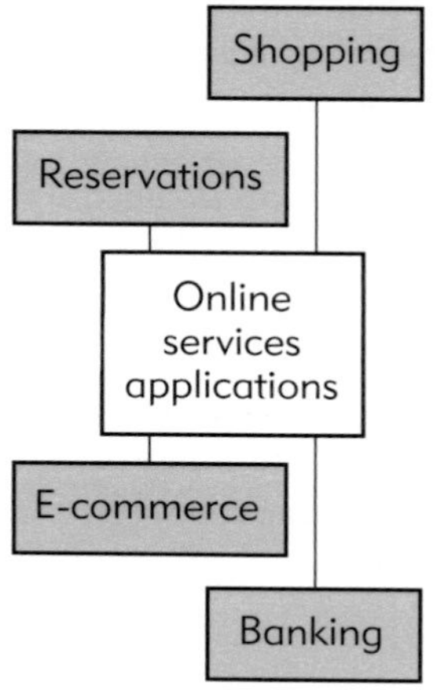

Figure 2.29 Online services

Services provided on the Internet or on electronic networks can be described as online services. They fall into four main categories:

- Shopping: visiting a virtual shop, selecting and paying for goods electronically.
- Reservations: Booking and paying for tickets or flights online. Real-time processing of transactions is used to ensure that tickets and flights are not double booked.
- E-commerce: Defined as 'conducting business transactions over electronic networks'.
- Banking: Customers bank online using the Internet or telephone banking. They can maintain their own accounts without having to pay bank fees, such as setting up standing orders and transferring money from one account to another. Customers are even paid by their employers using EFT.

Effects on a business

Advantages	Disadvantages
• Worldwide client access so a business can have a larger customer base, both locally and globally. • The business can communicate with customers immediately, such as supplying product information and specifications (including graphics) through online electronic catalogues. • The use of the Internet allows a business to advertise new products and current promotions cheaper than in national newspapers. • New clients can be found without the need for employing salespeople. • Product information can be updated frequently and immediately.	• Home working can lead to a lack of human interaction between employees which can lead to feelings of isolation. • Modern technology can be expensive to purchase and maintain.

Advantages	Disadvantages
• Provides a quick and cheap method of doing market research on customer views. • The impact of the Internet can be assessed by counting visits to the site. • Less staff and overheads because no premises are required to sell stock.	

Effects on customers

Advantages	Disadvantages
• The Internet is now readily available on a home PC with cheap local call access anywhere in the world. • Growing amount of information (electronic catalogues) on a wide variety of topics. • Valuable learning resource for customers because Internet skills may be required for their jobs. • A range of product reviews can be obtained before deciding to make a purchase. • Goods are normally cheaper than buying on the high street. Customers normally get free delivery when they purchase over a certain value/amount. • You can buy goods from anywhere in the world which means you are not restricted to shopping in your own town or city. • Search engines can assist the user to precisely locate what they need • The multimedia format of the Internet makes it attractive and easier for customers to use. • Other services, such as e-mail, can be used by customers to request more information. • Customers can shop 24 hours a day, seven days a week.	• No guarantee the information on a website is accurate or up to date. • Large amount of undesirable material, such as pornography, is readily available. • Large dial-up telephone bills can result if Internet is used during peak hours. • Excessive time on the Internet could result in a lack of interaction with others, leading to a decline in social skills. • Going online runs the risk of hackers gaining access to your personal details or downloading a virus onto your hard drive. • Using only a keyword or inappropriate searching techniques in a search engine may make it difficult to find appropriate information. • Many customers are worried about credit card fraud when buying goods.

Revision questions

1 Expand the following acronyms/abbreviations and give a brief explanation of how each one is used in a computer system.

Acronym/abbreviation	Explanation
EFT	
POS	
EPOS	
EFTPOS	
ATM	
PIN	
ADC	

2 Complete the following table and list the devices as specified.

Input devices in an EFTPOS	Output devices at an EFTPOS	Processing devices at an EFTPOS

3 How does an EFT make use of barcodes?

4 Place the following statements in order to describe what happens when a customer pays for goods at an EFTPOS.

A PIN entered
B Receipt printed
C Authorisation check
D Card swiped/placed into 'chip and pin' terminal

5 A supermarket makes use of EFTPOS. List **three** advantages to the customer and **three** advantages to the vendor of using this system.

6 Banks and building societies make use of ATMs.

a List **four** facilities provided at an ATM.
b Explain the security checks used at an ATM.
c What is the advantage to the customer of using an ATM?
d What is the advantage to the bank of using an ATM?

7 Smart chips and magnetic stripes are used in credit cards.
  a How does a smart card differ from a magnetic stripe card?
  b What is the advantage of having a smart chip in a credit card?
  c Give three uses of smart chip technology.

8 a Which following items of data are contained on a barcode?
    A price, product code and manufacturer code
    B price, country of origin and manufacturer code
    C number in stock, country of origin and manufacturer code
    D Product code, country of origin and manufacturer code
  b Batch processing is:
    A suitable when a fast response is required
    B suitable for processing small amounts of data
    C suitable for processing large volumes of data
    D suitable for storing large volumes of data

9 Electricity bills are created using batch processing.
  a What is the role of the master file in a batch processing system?
  b What is the role of the transaction file in a batch processing system?
  c Why is the transaction file sorted into the same order as the master file?
  d List two items of output from a batch processing system.

10 What special equipment is required to make use of a virtual reality system?

11 a List three different ways in which virtual reality is used.
  b What is the advantage of using virtual reality for training surgeons?

12 Computers are used in control systems.
  a Feedback occurs when:
    A the output from a system affects the input
    B the input from a system affects the output
    C the input to the system is processed by a computer
    D the input to the system is recorded
  b The process of feedback involves:
    A recording data, comparing values and taking action
    B recording data, storing data and taking action
    C storing data, taking action and comparing values
    D storing data, comparing values, taking action
  c Which of the following is not an advantage of using computers to log data:
    A It is more accurate than a human collecting data.
    B It is safer than a human collecting data.
    C It means data can be collected over a period of time and then analysed by special/dedicated software.

13 Describe **three** ways in which computers are used in control. For each one show the input, processing and output.

14 Online services are provided in a variety of areas. List these areas.

15 List **three** advantages to the user of using online services.

16 List **three** advantages to the vendor or company of using online services.

Examination questions

1 Elaine is booking flights for a holiday. A screenshot of her booking so far is shown below.

Figure 2.30 Airline online booking form (1)

a What type of processing is used to complete the booking? Tick the correct answer.

Real-time processing ☐

Batch processing ☐

[1]

b Why is it necessary for this transaction to be processed immediately?

[1]

This is a screenshot of Elaine's booking before she has paid for the flights.

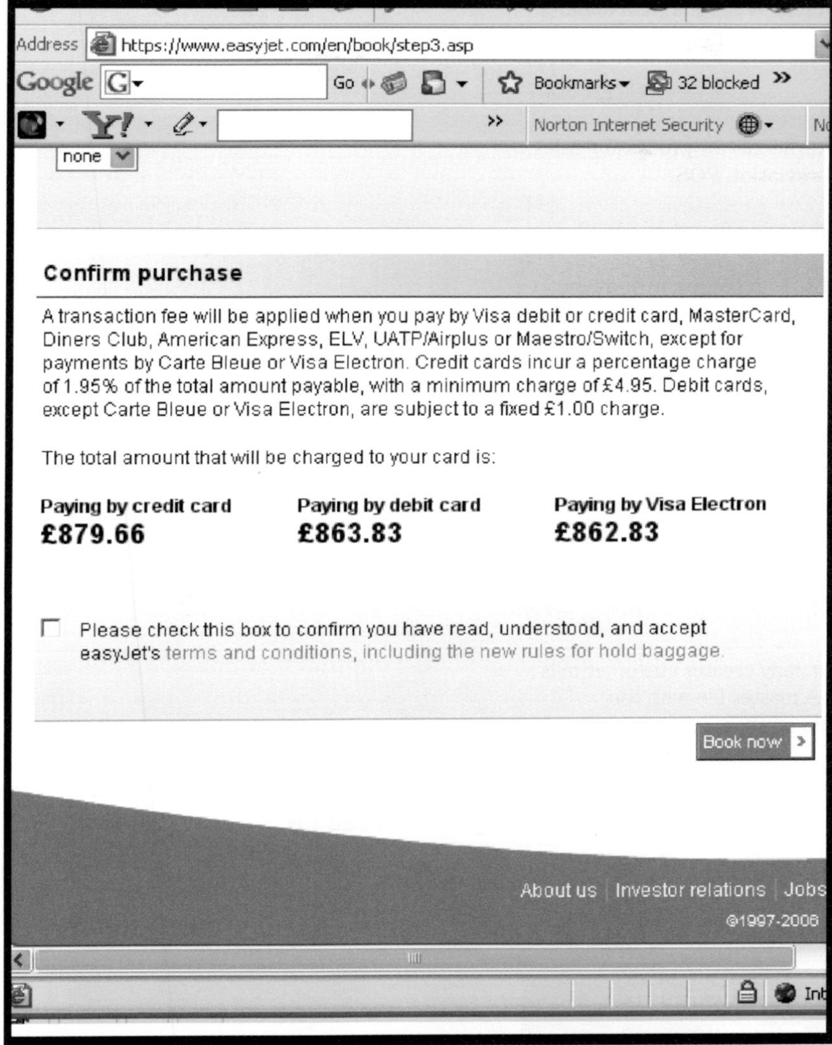

Figure 2.31 Airline online booking form (2)

c Which **two** features will help Elaine decide that this is a secure site? [2]

d List **two** advantages to the company of having a website that allows flight booking. [2]

CCEA 2007

2 **a** Fill in the blank spaces using some of the words below.

analogue	**digital**	**sensor**
ADC	**PC**	**thermometer**

A feedback loop is an important part of many control systems. A _______ records physical data which is in _______ form. This data is then converted to _______ form using an _______ so the computer can work with it. [4]

b John is using data logging equipment in a science laboratory, What is data logging? [2]

c Give **one** advantage to John of using a data logger instead of conducting the experiment manually. [1]

d John has set up his experiment. He wants to create a graph to display the temperature of water as it cools. He will use a data logging interval of two minutes. What is a data logging interval?

[1]

CCEA 2007

3 Supermarkets use POS terminals for processing sales.

a **i** Expand the abbreviation POS.

[1]

ii Name **one** input device found at a POS.

[1]

iii Give **two** benefits to a company of having a POS system.

[2]

EFT can also take place at the terminal.

b Give **one** advantage to the customer of using EFT.

[1]

Supermarkets link their computer system on a LAN. They communicate with their distribution centres using a WAN.

c Expand the acronym WAN.

[1]

CCEA 2007

4 The EnergyFlow gas company creates customer bills using batch processing. A master file with the following fields holds data on their customers.

Customer number	Name	Address	Last meter reading	Current meter reading	Units used	Total

Their transaction file has the following fields:

Customer number	Current meter reading

a **i** What is a master file?

[2]

ii What is a transaction file?

[2]

b **i** Customers' current meter readings are recorded on OMR sheets. Give **one** advantage to the company of using these?

[1]

ii Why must the transaction file be sorted into the same order as the master file before processing?

[1]

c List **two** outputs created in batch processing. [2]

CCEA 2007

5 Supermarkets use barcode scanners to enter product details at the Electronic Point of Sale (EPOS) Terminal.

a Circle **two** output devices in the EPOS system shown below. [2]

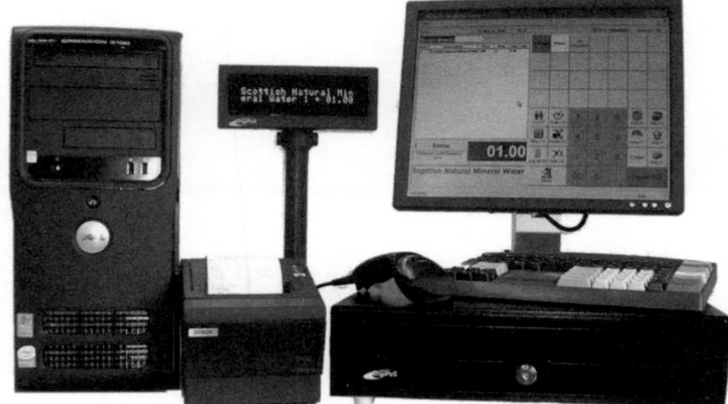

Figure 2.32 EPOS system

b Barcodes contain a check digit. Name **two** other items of data held on a supermarket barcode. [2]

c Put the following processes in order using the numbers 1–6 to show what happens when an item is scanned at an EPOS.

Process	Order
Till beeps if match	
Price retrieved from store database	
Barcode is scanned using laser scanner	
Receipt printed	
Check digit is calculated and compared with scanned one	
Price displayed	

[6]

6 David has built a new conservatory. His heating system uses an embedded computer to keep the temperature between 24°C and 28°C at all times. The diagram below shows the system he uses.

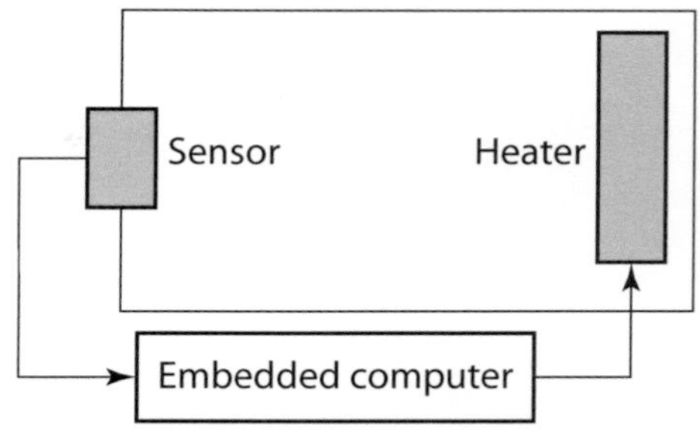

a What type of sensor is used in this system? [1]

b Explain how this system uses feedback to control the temperature in the room. [2]

c Name **two** other devices in the home that use embedded computers for control. [2]

d Give **two** other examples where feedback is used to control a process outside the home. [2]

CCEA 2007

3

Unit C3: Implications of ICT for individuals, organisations and society

This chapter will cover the implications of ICT for individuals, organisations and society. You need to understand the implications in the following areas:

- education
- employment
- health and safety issues
- home and leisure
- data protection legislation

You will need to answer questions using examples from your everyday living and be aware of how ICT is used today.

Acronyms and abbreviations

Acronym/abbreviation	Meaning
CD-ROM	Compact Disk – Read-Only Memory
CAL	Computer-Assisted Learning
MIDI	Musical Instrument Digital Interface
DVD	Digital Versatile Disk
LAN	Local Area Network
WAN	Wide Area Network
C2K	Classroom 2000
VLE	Virtual Learning Environment
WAP	Wireless Application Protocol
PDA	Personal Digital Assistant
RSI	Repetitive Strain Injury
ELF	Extremely Low Frequency
LCD	Liquid Crystal Display
MPEG	Motion Picture Expert Group
DV	Digital Video
USB	Universal Serial Bus

EFT	Electronic Funds Transfer
SET	Secure Electronic Transaction
FAST	Federation Against Software Theft
IP	Internet Protocol

Definitions required

Term	Definition
Generic software	The software is appropriate in a number of different applications, such as word processing.
Multimedia	Human–computer interaction (HCI) involving the integration of text, graphics, voice and video.
Firewall	A firewall is an ICT device or a piece of software which controls traffic to and from a network.
E-learning	Learning provided and supported using ICT, such as an online interactive course whereby all learning and assessment is done via a computer system.
Intranet	Provides a similar service as the Internet except it is controlled within an organisation. Each user must have authorisation to use the service.
Teleworking	The use of ICT to enable people to work from home.
Ergonomics	All aspects of a job, from the physical stresses it places on joints and muscles to environmental factors which can affect hearing, vision, and general comfort and health.
Digibox	A term used to describe a digital receiver for satellite, terrestrial or cable television. May contain a decoder.
File compression	The technique of reducing the space required by a large file.
MP3 file	A compressed audio file which can maintain the quality of the sound.
Firewire	A type of cable for transferring data to and from digital devices, such as a digital camera, at high speed.
E-commerce	The use of the Internet for commercial tasks such as shopping.
Digital signature	A code that guarantees a sender's identity. If an unauthorised person decrypts it, the digital signature will be altered. This means that the recipient will recognise that the code has been decrypted.
Digital certificate	An electronic identification that confirms that the user is an authentic person. A bank will issue this certificate which contains information about the user.
Software licence	When software is purchased a licence is included which states the conditions in which the software can be used. They tend to be classified as single user or multi-user.
Data Commissioner (now 'Information Commissioner')	Person responsible for enforcing the Data Protection Act, and for promoting and making the general public aware of their rights under the Act.
Data Controller	The person in a company who is responsible for controlling the way in which personal data is processed under the Data Protection Act.
Data Subject	The individual who is the subject of the personal data under the Data Protection Act.
Personal data	Concerns a living person who can be identified from the data.

Education

The impact of ICT on education

- The twenty-first century classroom makes use of technology, contributing to teaching and learning.
- Open ended (or generic) software, such as Microsoft Office, allows pupils to use tools to create high quality and well-presented homework and coursework.
- Interactive subject-specific learning materials are produced on CD-ROM.
- Multimedia software presents on-screen moving pictures and sounds.
- Special subject-specific packages such as *Geometry Inventor* in mathematics can assist teachers and pupils.
- Computer-Assisted Learning (CAL) packages can teach a topic in a multimedia environment. They can monitor learners' progress, and allow them to study at their own pace.
- Science and technology subjects make use of data-logging equipment, including sensors.
- CD writers and MIDI assist in learning and producing music.
- DVD technology provides learners with interactive films and real-life learning situations.
- A data projector can be used with an interactive whiteboard, allowing pupils to interact with the computer by pressing or clicking on the board.
- Technology can also assist learners with special educational needs.
- Accessibility tools such as Microsoft's Magnifier magnify text so that sight-impaired learners can read it.
- On-screen keyboards assist learners with low mobility – characters can be typed by simply rolling the mouse over the letter.
- Concept keyboards and tracker ball mouse devices can help those with limited mobility.
- Voice recognition software can be used to understand spoken word.
- Braille keyboards and printers can assist blind learners.

The Internet in education

- A school LAN usually has a WAN connection that allows access to the Internet.
- Search engines provide pupils with a powerful research facility using the Internet – using conventional libraries to reference information can be a slower task.
- Schools use a firewall to ensure that the content accessed by pupils is appropriate.
- Schools in Northern Ireland are connected to a WAN which is managed by C2K.

Communication technologies in education

- Communication technologies provide opportunities for e-learning.
- Pupils and teachers can use e-mail as a means of communicating.
- Video conferencing allows pupils to take part in two-way visual communication.
- Pupils can exchange ideas interactively and produce joint projects regardless of where their schools are geographically located.
- Bulletin boards and controlled interactive text-based discussion (similar to chat rooms) are used in schools.
- E-portfolios allow pupils to create and maintain an electronic collection of their projects and personal data.
- Pupils can access their documents from school using their home computer.
- Virtual Learning Environments (VLEs) are used in many universities to deliver their courses, allowing lecturers to monitor and assess students' work.

Employment

The impact of ICT on employment

- ICT is now a key element of our working lives and has led to changes in the way we do our jobs.
- Robots are used in manufacturing to do jobs which are highly repetitive and skilled, such as paint spraying in car factories.
- Office workers make use of applications software packages to produce documents and of technologies to communicate, such as intranets.
- Portable technology like laptops allows more people to take work home.
- Employees can be contacted at anytime and anywhere using mobile telephones or PDAs, resulting in boundaries between home and work becoming less defined.
- Businesses who want to operate in the global marketplace must be available 24 hours a day because of the time difference between countries. This allows companies to employ a global workforce.

Job displacement, retraining and job creation

- Many manual jobs have been replaced by ICT systems, such as filing clerks being replaced by databases.
- Many workers feel that they are becoming de-skilled because their role in the workplace has changed, such as bank cashiers doing a different job than they used to.
- As new technologies emerge, people require retraining.

- In all areas of working life there is a continual need to update skills creating a life-long learning environment.
- New technologies have also created new jobs, such as software engineers and web designers.

Home-based employment

- The use of communications technology has made working from home a viable option.
- Employees can stay in touch with the office by using e-mail, video conferencing and WAP-enabled hand-held devices like PDAs.
- Employees can also log on to their company's intranet from home.
- Working from home like this is called 'teleworking'.
- People who work from home like this are called 'teleworkers'.

Figure 3.1 Teleworking

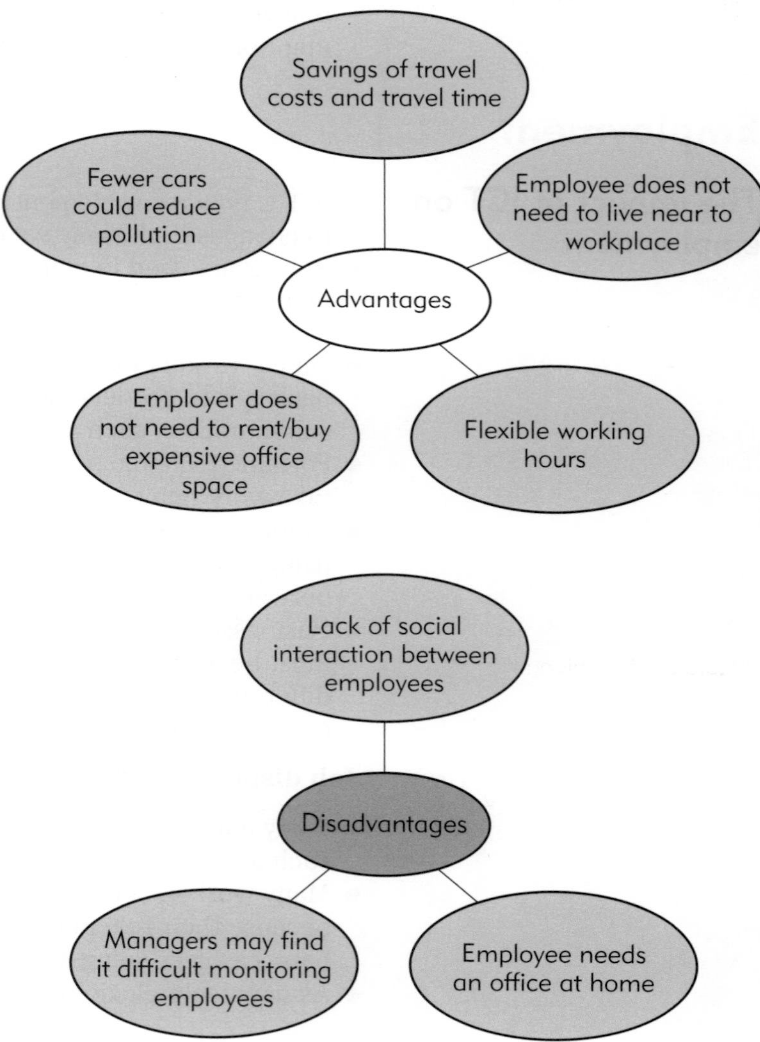

Health and safety issues

- Health problems and injuries can arise when using computers.
- Employers are responsible for providing a safe working environment.
- There are standards expected in areas such as:
  - lighting
  - furniture
  - noise
  - hardware and software
  - temperature control.

Repetitive Strain Injury (RSI)

RSI refers to straining muscles in the neck, shoulders, arms and hands due to constant use.

Figure 3.2 Minimising the risk of RSI

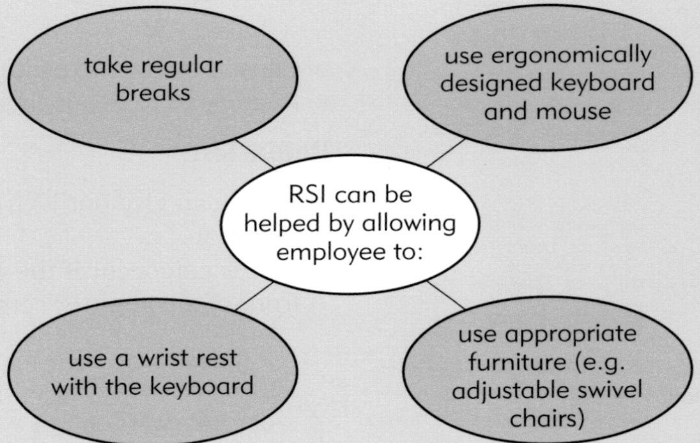

Back pain

The problem can be related to the position of a person at the computer.

Figure 3.3 Minimising the risk of back pain

Eyestrain

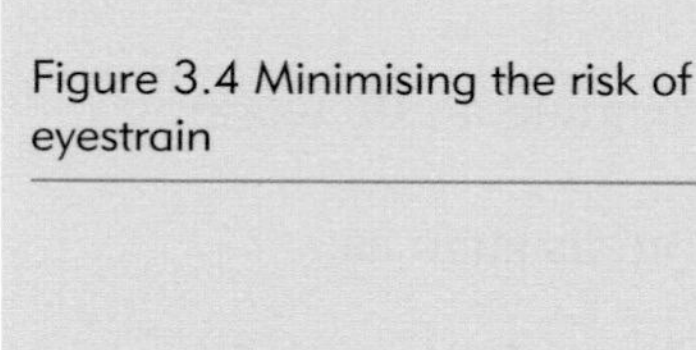
Figure 3.4 Minimising the risk of eyestrain

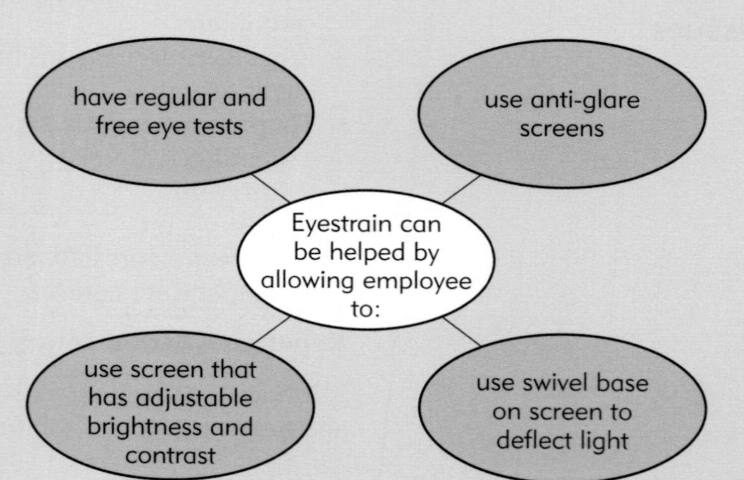

- Caused by over exposure to computer screens.
- It can lead to headaches and deterioration in eyesight.

Radiation

- VDUs can give out Extremely Low Frequency (ELF) radiation.
- Illness can occur if the user is working for long periods in front of a computer screen.

Figure 3.5 Minimising the risk of radiation illness

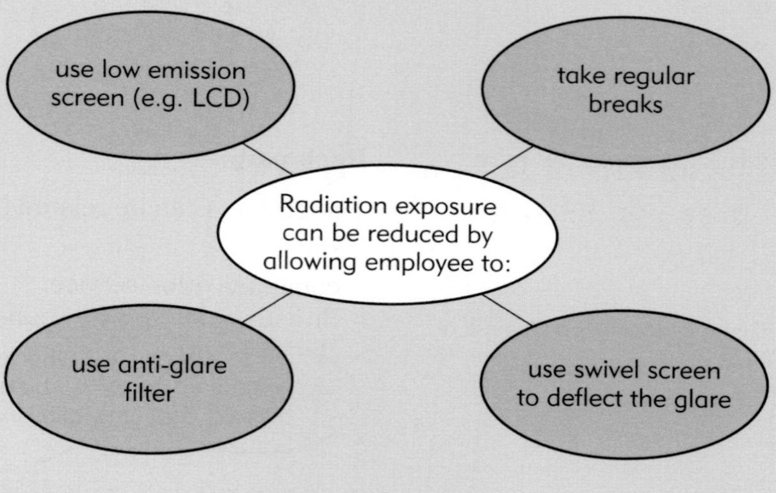

Safety in the workplace

A safe workplace means that employees will not have accidents.

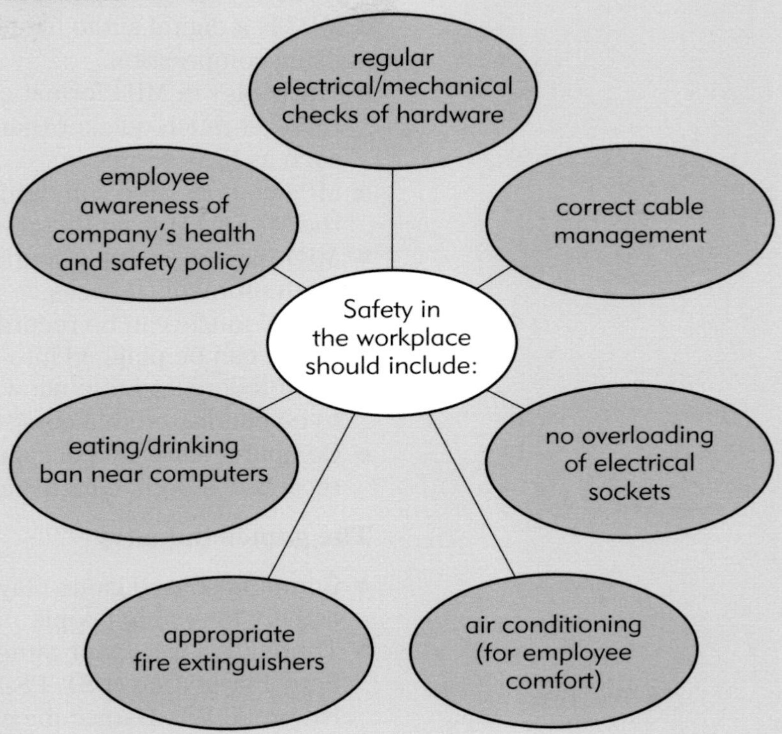

Figure 3.6 Safety in the workplace

Home and leisure

The impact of ICT on home and leisure

Digital TV

- Advances in technology, like the development of broadband, have created a fully integrated home communication service.
- Provides high quality sound and pictures.
- More television channels available.
- Electronic programme guides to provide information on each channel.
- 'Pay to view' and subscription packages available.
- Viewers can record one channel while watching another.
- Interactive TV available allowing activities such as home shopping.

The music industry

- Modern music is created and recorded digitally making the files very large – CDs are ideal for storing this data.

- People use the Internet to download music using MP3 technology.
- MP3 players are small in size, large in capacity and relatively cheap to purchase.
- MP3 is a digital audio file format for storing music files, using compression.
- Music files in MP3 format can be downloaded from the Internet much quicker than music files in other formats such as WAV format.
- MP4 compression standards are now being developed by the MPEG (Moving Pictures Expert Group).
- MP4 players can play sound and pictures or movies. They are multimedia devices.
- Digital music can be recorded using MIDI instruments which can be plugged into a PC.
- MIDI technology also allows several musical instruments to be connected to a computer.
- Computer software packages allow digital music to be recorded, stored, edited and played back through speakers.

The games industry

- Computer-based game playing is a very popular leisure activity for young people.
- There are a variety of game consoles available including Sony Playstation (PS1, PS2 and PS3), Microsoft X-box, Nintendo Wii, Gamecube and Gameboy Advanced.
- Game consoles use a variety of peripherals such as a joystick, a driving console, a game pad, a dance mat etc.
- Games can be played online between players all over the world.
- Users can experience realistic conditions using specialised head gear and gloves.
- Mobile phones are also used to play downloaded games.

The video industry

- Digital Video (DV) cameras are a method of recording movies in digital format on a digital video tape.
- Movies can then be transferred directly to a PC for editing, using a USB cable or firewire.
- Firewire is a special cable allowing the immediate transferal of digital video to a computer.
- Older analogue video recordings can be converted to digital format using a video digitiser.
- The development of DVD and video compression has made the storage of digital movies much easier.
- Movies stored on DVD have been compressed using MPEG format.

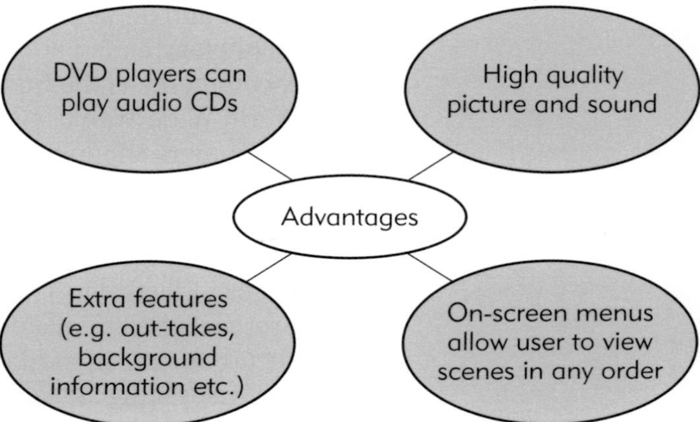

Figure 3.7 Using DVDs

Shopping

- More customers are using credit or debit cards to purchase goods.
- Money is transferred between accounts using EFT (Electronic Funds Transfer).

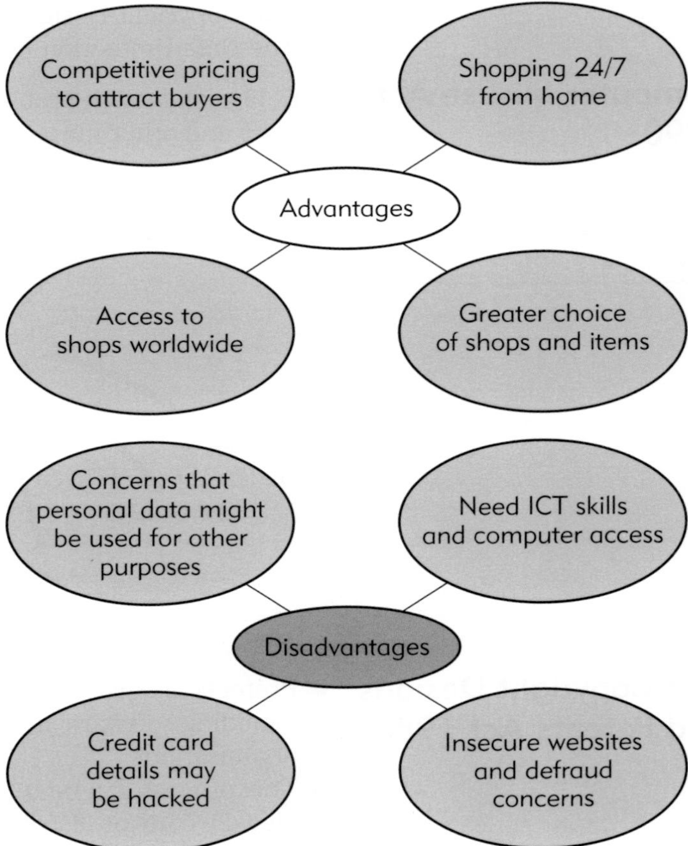

Figure 3.8 Online shopping

- Credit and debit cards make use of current 'chip and pin' technology aimed at cutting down on credit card fraud.
- E-commerce is the buying and selling of goods on the World Wide Web.
- Consumers shopping online have access to all the major stores 24 hours a day.
- Companies use data encryption techniques to secure against unauthorised access when paying for goods.
- Secure Electronic Transaction (SET) is a standard protocol used to make online purchases much more secure for credit card users.
- SET uses a digital signature and a digital certificate to confirm a customer's identity and their ability to pay.
- An icon (a closed padlock) is displayed at the bottom of the web page to indicate that SET is being used.

Computers and the law

The main laws include:

- The Computer Misuse Act of 1990
- The Copyright Designs and Patents Act of 1988
- The Data Protection Act 1998

Computer Misuse Act 1990

This law deals with problems involving hacking, planting viruses and other nuisances.

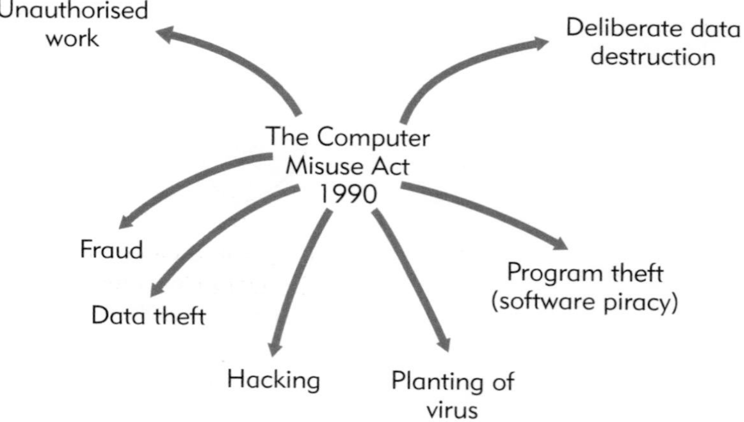

Figure 3.9 The Computer Misuse Act 1990 makes many practices illegal

The Copyright Designs and Patents Act 1988

- Protects against unauthorised reproduction of materials including software and documentation owned by organisations.
- This process can be referred to as 'piracy' whereby people illegally copy or distribute someone else's work.

- Organisations such as FAST (The Federation Against Software Theft) help protect against illegal use of software.
- Software on a network requires a software licence.
- Other ICT areas where copyright can be breached include:
  - using graphics, music or text downloaded from the Internet without acknowledgement and/or permission
  - copying materials on CD or DVD and distributing them
  - using existing software materials or ideas as your own
  - using unlicensed software.

Data Protection Act 1998

- Data security and data privacy are important issues for organisations which store personal data.
- Before the Data Protection Act organisations were able to share personal data.

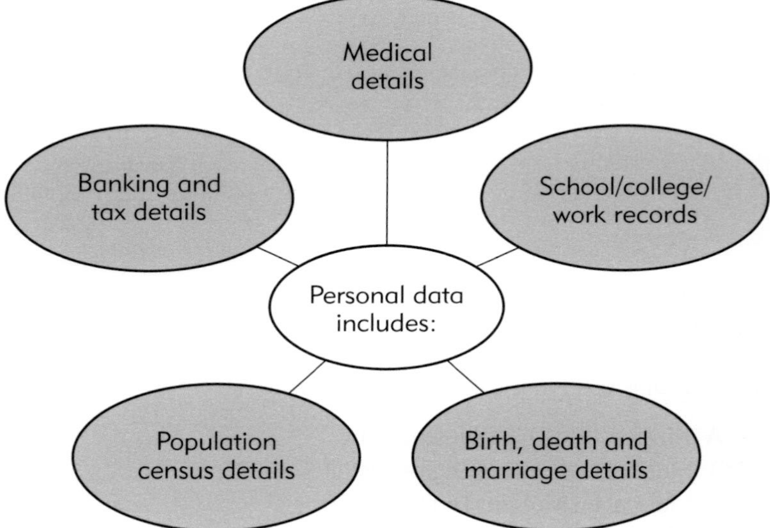

Figure 3.10 Some data covered by the Data Protection Act

- If an organisation uses personal data, it is now a legal requirement for it to register its intent and comply with the principles of the Data Protection Act.
- The Data Commissioner (now 'Information Commissioner') is responsible for enforcing the Act.
- Organisations employ Data Controllers who are responsible for the way in which personal data is processed.
- There are eight principles which companies must comply with. Personal data:
  - should be processed fairly and lawfully with the consent of the Data Subject
  - should be used for the specified purpose only
  - should be adequate and relevant for its intended purpose
  - should be accurate and up to date.

- should not be kept for longer than necessary
- should be processed in accordance with the rights of the Data Subject
- should be held securely, with no unauthorised access
- should not be transferred to other countries that do not comply with any form of data protection laws.

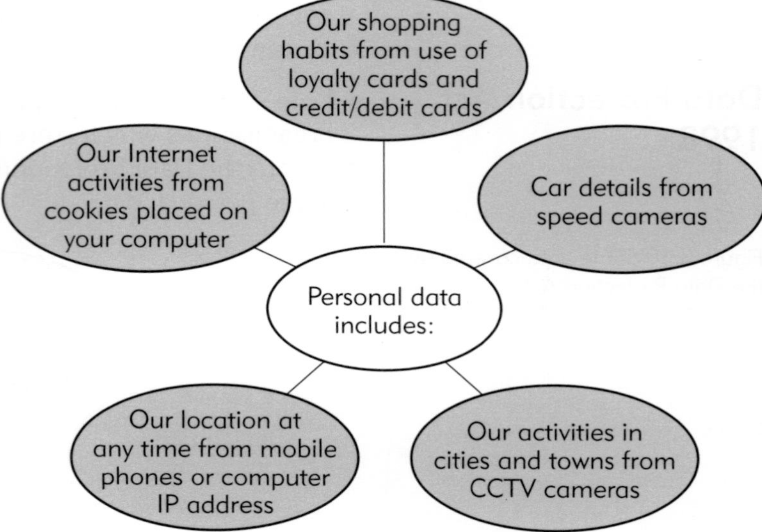

Figure 3.11 Some data is regularly collected without us knowing

Revision questions

1 A MIDI is used in music. What does MIDI stand for?

A Musical Into Digital Instrument
B Musical Instrument Digital Install
C Musical Instrument Digital Interface
D Musical Interface Digital Instrument

2 Which of the following is an area of health and safety in ICT?

A E-learning
B Data security
C Ergonomics
D Data privacy

3 RSI is an injury caused by excess use of a computer. What does RSI stand for?

A Repetitive Strain Injury
B Recurring Strain Injury
C Repetitive Standing Injury
D Random Strain Injury

4 Which of these is an advantage to a teleworking employee?

A No need to travel to work
B Flexible working life
C Can save money on transport costs
D All of the above

5 Which of these is a disadvantage of using ICT in education?

A Online information access to the Internet.
B Restricting learner access to parts of the network.
C Learner access to e-mail.
D Being able to download computer games.

6 Which of the following is not a principle of the Data Protection Act?

A Personal data should be accurate and up to date.
B Personal data should not be kept for longer than necessary.
C Personal data should be held securely.
D Personal data should be held for any reasonable purpose.

7 Which law makes it illegal to plant a virus on a computer system?

A The Data Protection Act
B The Computer Misuse Act
C The Copyright Designs and Patents Act
D All of the above

8 The Internet can be used to purchase goods online, pay by credit card and have the goods delivered to your home. Which of the following is an advantage of shopping online?

A Customers are concerned about fraud.
B Customers can shop 24 hours a day, seven days a week.
C Customers have no access to the Internet.
D There is no need to worry about their personal details.

9 Which of the following best describes Firewire?

A A type of cable for transferring data to and from digital devices at high speed.
B Software to block an unwanted virus entering a network.
C A cable that has over heated due to large data files.
D A wireless link between two devices.

10 Which of the following is not a recognised technique of ensuring data security?

A Passwords
B Chip and PIN
C Data validation
D Data encryption

True or false?

1 EFT allows money to be transferred from one bank to another.

2 Teleworking is using ICT to work from your company office.

3 Due to advances in ICT the overall number of jobs has decreased.

4 ICT in education has the potential to provide benefits to learners with disabilities.

5 Robots are used in car factories to help assemble new cars.

6 One way in which ICT is affecting people is the continual need for training.

7 Developments in communications technology have made working from home a viable option.

8 A disadvantage of using teleworking is the lack of social interaction between employees.

9 Using anti-glare screens can reduce eyestrain among ICT users.

10 A Secure Electronic Transaction involves both a digital signature and a digital certificate.

Match a word to a statement

A backup	**B** piracy	**C** Firewire	**D** copyright
E Digital signature	**F** MP3 file	**G** compression	**H** e-commerce

1 A type of cable for transferring data at high speeds from other devices.

2 An electronic ID that confirms that the user is an authentic user.

3 A compressed audio file.

4 The technique for reducing the space required by large files.

5 Regular copying and storing of data to prevent loss of data.

6 A form of protection for the original programmer who wrote the software.

7 Doing business over the Internet.

8 Unauthorised reproduction of computer software and documentation.

Examination questions

1 It is claimed that digital TV (DTV) gives CD-quality sound and a better quality picture than analogue TV. Give **two** other features of DTV.

[2]

CCEA 2003

2 Many shoppers are offered discounts if they have a store card. According to the Data Protection Act the owners of the stores have to register before they can issue cards.

a Why is this?

[2]

b Give **three** measures of protection the Act gives to the shopper.

[3]

CCEA 2003

3 Some people hack into data on the World Wide Web.

a What does it mean to hack into data?

[2]

b Which Government Act is meant to deal with hacking?

[1]

CCEA 2003

4 **a** Describe **one** advantage of online shopping for the retailer and **one** advantage for the buyer.

[2]

b Give **one** reason why people may be worried about shopping on the Internet.

[1]

CCEA 2003

5 Describe **two** benefits a school, college or organisation may gain from having an intranet.

[2]

CCEA 2003

6 In 1992, a new European directive came into force affecting everyone who works with VDUs and computers. It is aimed to safeguard the health and safety of everyone who works with this equipment. List **five** measures that could be taken to safeguard the health and safety of computer users in schools.

[5]

CCEA 2003

7 It is sometimes said that the Information Technology Revolution is affecting the way everybody works. Write a report describing **four** ways in which ICT has changed the way people work.

[5]

CCEA 2003

8 Smith's superstore keeps details about its customers. A customer, Mrs Greene, notices that her date of birth and her occupation have been recorded incorrectly. She decides to write to Smith's superstore about this, reminding them of the Data Protection Act.

a State **two** points that she could make about her rights as a Data Subject.

[2]

b Explain **one** responsibility that Smith's Superstore have as the Data User under the Data Protection Act.

[1]

If Mrs Greene is not happy with the response she receives from Smith's Superstore, she can complain to the Data Commissioner.

c What is the role of the Data Commissioner?

[2]

Mrs Greene arrives home and her son John is playing a music CD. The CD has been copied by a friend using a CD Rewriter.

d Which law has John broken?

[1]

CCEA 2004

9 Many people worry about privacy issues when using the Internet. Certain measures are in place to provide protection for users. How do the following provide protection for the users?

[6]

a digital signatures
b SET
c encryption

CCEA 2004

10 Using computers incorrectly for a long period of time can lead to injuries, such as RSI, back problems and eye problems.

a What is RSI?

[1]

b Suggest **two** measures that can be taken to prevent RSI.

[2]

c Suggest **two** measures that can be taken to prevent eye problems.

[2]

CCEA 2004

11 New technologies have had a major impact on our lifestyles. There have been many changes in the music, leisure and entertainment industries.

a Give **four** examples of how new technology has made changes to the music, leisure and entertainment industries.

[6]

b ICT is also changing the way in which we learn. Describe how each of the following new technologies might be used to support teaching and learning.

i CD-ROM
ii intranet
iii Internet
iv e-mail.

[6]

CCEA 2004

12 The Internet has opened up a new world of cyber shopping, e-shopping and e-commerce, resulting in a new experience for the shopper and the retailer. More and more stores are giving us the opportunity of shopping online.

a What is meant by shopping online?

[1]

b State **one** advantage for the retailer of shopping online.

[1]

c State **two** advantages for the customer of shopping online.

[2]

d Give **one** reason why a customer may be worried about the security of shopping in this way.

[1]

e Give **one** way retailers make customers feel that their system is safe from misuse.

[1]

f Many supermarkets allow customers to use a loyalty card or a store card. The customer gives personal details to the supermarket when applying for the card. Give **three** ways the customer is protected under the Data Protection Act from misuse of information given to the supermarket.

[3]

CCEA 2005

13 Alison runs a small publishing business. She employs five people and wants to make sure they are working in a safe environment.

a List and give the cause of **three** possible injuries which employees could suffer because of working at the computer for a long time.

[6]

Injury	Cause

b List **three** ways in which Alison can help prevent her employees from having health problems in the workplace.

[3]

CCEA 2005

14 ICT can be used by employers to allow teleworking.

[2]

a Give **two** advantages for an employee of teleworking.

[2]

b Jones and Sons Ltd are a Belfast-based multimedia design company. They have many people asking them to do work but are finding that they cannot find people in the Belfast area with the right skills. Anne, the Production Manager, has suggested employing teleworkers. As Anne, write a short paragraph explaining the advantages and disadvantages for Jones and Sons Ltd if they include teleworkers on their staff.

[5]

CCEA 2005

15 A company produces a range of greeting cards. The company keeps information on customers and must abide by the Data Protection Act.

a List **two** principles of this Act.

[2]

b The company has been offered a teleworking contract. List **three** ways in which its work pattern may change if it accepts this contract.

[3]

CCEA 2006

16 A mail order company uses computers to hold data on its staff and customers.

a Give **two** reasons why people worry about data held about them on computers.

[2]

b Who must the company register with before they can hold this data on computers?

[1]

c When the company is e-mailing customer account details they use security to prevent a hacker from accessing it. Explain the term 'hacker'.

[1]

d Digital signatures and SET can help keep transactions more secure.

i What is a digital signature?

ii What is SET?

[4]

CCEA 2006

17 Our lifestyle and leisure time have been changed because of computers and the Internet. Explain how we use computers and the Internet for leisure and to improve our lifestyle.

[5]

CCEA 2006

4

Acronyms and abbreviations

ADC	Analogue to Digital Converter
ADSL	Asymmetric Digital Subscriber Line
ASCII	American Standard Code for Information Interchange
ATM	Automatic Teller Machine
Bcc	Blind Carbon Copy
bit	Binary DigIT
C2K	Classroom 2000
CAL	Computer-Assisted Learning
Cc	Carbon Copy
CD-R	Compact Disk-Recordable
CD-ROM	Compact Disk-Read-Only Memory
CD-RW	Compact Disk-Rewritable
CPU	Central Processing Unit
dpi	Dots Per Inch
DVD	Digital Versatile Disk
EFT	Electronic Funds Transfer
EFTPOS	Electronic Funds Transfer Point Of Sale
ELF	Extremely Low Frequency
EPOS	Electronic Point Of Sale
FAST	Federation Against Software Theft
GB	Gigabyte
GUI	Graphical User Interface
HTML	HyperText Mark-up Language
IP	Internet Protocol
ISDN	Integrated Services Digital Network
ISP	Internet Service Provider
JPEG	Joint Photographic Experts Group
LAN	Local Area Network
LCD	Liquid Crystal Display
MB	Megabyte
MIDI	Musical Instrument Digital Interface
MPEG	Motion Picture Expert Group
OCR	Optical Character Recognition
OMR	Optical Mark Recognition
PC	Personal Computer
PDA	Personal Digital Assistant
PIN	Personal Identification Number
POS	Point Of Sale
ppm	Pages Per Minute
PSTN	Public Switched Telephone Network
RAM	Random Access Memory
ROM	Read-Only Memory
RSI	Repetitive Strain Injury
RTF	Rich Text Format
SET	Secure Electronic Transaction
SVGA	Super Video Graphics Array
URL	Uniform Resource Locator
VDU	Visual Display Unit
VLE	Virtual Learning Environment
WAN	Wide Area Network
WAP	Wireless Application Protocol
WIMP	Windows, Icons, Menus, Pointers
WORM	Write-Once Read-Many
WWW	World Wide Web
WYSIWYG	What You See Is What You Get

Answers to questions

Chapter 1

Revision questions

Multiple choice

1 C 2 A 3 D 4 D 5 B 6 C
7 A 8 C 9 C 10 C

True or false?

1 T 2 T 3 T 4 F 5 F 6 T
7 T 8 T 9 F 10 T

Match a word to a statement

1 H 2 G 3 B 4 C 5 E 6 D
7 F 8 A

Chapter C2a

Acronym/ abbreviation	Expansion	Explanation
CPU	Central Processing Unit	All processing occurs here. It is made of ALU, Control Unit, memory.
VDU	Visual Display Unit	Output device
CD-ROM	Compact Disk–Read-Only Memory	Optical storage device
DVD	Digital Versatile Disk	Optical storage device
RAM	Random Access Memory	Volatile memory used to store temporary copies of files and the operating system whilst the computer is switched on.
ROM	Read-Only Memory	Non-volatile memory used to store the boot up program of the PC.
Bit	Binary Digit	Smallest unit of storage.
MB	Megabyte	1024 KB
GB	Gigabyte	1024 MB
LCD	Liquid Crystal Display	Output device, thinner than a cathode ray VDU.
dpi	Dots Per Inch	Number of dots used to print images on a printer. The more dots per inch, the higher the quality of the image.
OCR	Optical Character Recognition	A form of data capture that reads characters and turns them into digital data for processing.
SVGA	Super Video Graphics Array	A screen resolution.
ppm	Pages Per Minute	A measure of the speed of a printer.
CD-R	Compact Disk-Recordable	An optical storage device which can be written to only once, but read from many times.
CD-RW	Compact Disk-Rewritable	An optical storage device which can be written to and read from many times.
WORM	Write Once Read Many	Can only write to it once but it can be read many times.
GUI	Graphical User Interface	A user interface which makes use of WIMP to allow users to interact with a computer.
WIMP	Windows, Icons, Menus, Pointers	A GUI

Revision questions

1

2 a Memory used to hold programs and data that the user is using (e.g. Windows, Microsoft Word and the document being typed).

b Non-volatile memory – that is programs stored on ROM are permanent and the contents cannot be altered. It is used to store the 'boot up' program for Windows. This program runs automatically when the computer is turned on to load the operating system (such as Microsoft Windows XP).

c All processing of data occurs here. Processor speed is in gigahertz (GHz), typically 1.2 GHz.

3 bit / byte / character / kilobyte

4 byte / kilobyte / megabyte / gigabyte

5 a the operating system enables all of the hardware and software to work together / it also allows the user to interact with the computer system / Microsoft Windows Vista and Windows XP are operating systems / the operating system of a computer is stored on the hard disk whilst the computer is switched off.

b share time between processes and applications running on the computer / allocate memory effectively so that all processes have an adequate amount of memory to run / manage and communicate with all devices connected to the computer, this is sometimes done using drivers / provides a user interface for the user to communicate with the computer – the most popular type of interface is a Graphical User Interface (GUI)

c windows / icons / menus / pointers

6 1 The computer is switched on and a system configuration check is carried out.

2 A boot strap program held in ROM is executed. This tells the computer to load the operating system.

3 The operating system is then loaded into RAM from the hard disk.

7 Random Access Memory / volatile / Read-only Memory / non-volatile / operating system

8

Statement	Tick if true
RAM cannot be written to.	
Data in ROM is not lost when the computer is switched off.	✓
RAM can be written to but not read from.	
RAM can be written to and read from.	✓
ROM holds the operating system.	
ROM holds the program which boots up the computer.	✓

9 to process instructions faster

10

Purpose	Device
Entering large amounts of text into a computer	Keyboard
Playing computer games	Joystick
Using a GUI	Mouse
Weighing fruit and vegetables in a supermarket	Touch screen or concept keyboard
Converting hard copies of pictures into digital images	Scanner
Selecting options on a screen in a tourist information office	Touch screen
Moving the mouse cursor on a laptop	Tracker pad
Recording voice input for storage on a computer	Microphone

11 If text has been scanned it can be recognised as text on a word processor using optical character recognition (OCR) software.

12 E.g. concept keyboard – checkout / touch screen – fruit and vegetable counter / barcode reader – checkout

13 a C b B c B d C e B f D g B

14

Task	Printer	Two features
30 000 high quality letters	Laser	Fast, good images
A GCSE geography project	Ink-jet	Cheap to buy, expensive to run
A set of architect's plans	Plotter	Slow to produce output, produces good quality output
Producing a carbon copy invoice for a customer.	Dot matrix	Noisy, cheap to use

15 Cathode ray monitor: works in the same way as a television; bulky and takes up a lot of space.

TFT LCD monitor: much lighter and smaller than a CRT monitor: uses less power; uses LCD technology to create pixels; better for users in terms of health and safety; gives off less heat and is quieter; easily damaged by sharp objects.

16 Permanent storage of data or programs

17 floppy disk Zip disk CD-RW magnetic tape hard disk

18

	CD-R	CD-RW	CD-ROM
Capacity	700 MB	700 MB	700 MB
Purchased blank?	Yes	Yes	No
Can be written to many times?	No	Yes	No
Is used for?	Storing data / backup	Storing data in portable form	Storing software
Cost	Cheapest	More expensive than CD-R	

19 Magnetic tape: large storage capacity / cheap to buy

20 floppy disk / magnetic tape / Zip disk / hard disk (fastest)

21 CD-RW / CD-R / DVD-RW (highest storage capacity)

22 non-volatile / can be erased / has no moving parts. Used in memory cards, USB Flash drives, PDAs and mobile phones.

Chapter C2b Revision questions

1

Acronym/ abbreviation	Expansion	Explanation
ASCII	American Standard Code for Information Interchange	A standard code made up of a set of binary digits and representing a letter.
OCR	Optical Character Recognition	A scanner is used to scan text on a document into the computer. OCR software on the computer changes the letters into characters that can be edited on a computer.
OMR	Optical Mark Recognition	A scanner is used to scan marks on a specially designed document into the computer. OMR software changes the marks into meaningful data so that the computer can process it.

2 Data: raw facts and figures (e.g. 12, 4, 5) – there is no indication of what the numbers mean.

Information: data that has been processed and has meaning (e.g. 12 cm, 4 cm, 5 cm) – the data is given the meaning of length.

3 a

Field	Data type	Sample data
Title	Text	Mr
Forename	Text	John
Surname	Text	Black
Sex	Yes/No (Boolean)	M
Date of Birth	Date	12/12/00
Street	Text	1 Long road
Town	Text	Smalltown
Postcode	Text	BH5 1BR
Phone Number	Text	028776655996
Distance from the club	Integer/Numeric	2
Method of transport	Text	Car
Previous club	Text	Big town
Permission to use photographs	Yes/No	Y
Medical Conditions	Memo/Text	None
Parent's name	Text	Anne Black

4 b To uniquely identify each record in the database.

c More than one person could have the same surname.

6

Task	Validation check
To ensure a surname is less than 30 characters.	Length
To ensure that a value has been entered in the Key Field.	Presence
To ensure that a date has been entered in the following way: 12/12/99	Format
To ensure that a postcode has been entered correctly.	Format
To ensure that data entered is a number.	Type
To ensure a membership number is between 1000 and 2000.	Range

7 Proofreading:documents can be proofread to ensure that they contain correct and accurate information.

Double entry of data:data is keyed into the computer system twice by two different computer operators / the computer system compares the two sets of data / any mismatching data is rejected and must be re-entered.

8 The check digit is compared with the results of a calculation using the code. If the results of the calculation do not match the check digit, the code has to be input again.

9 Data is input into the computer directly using a method such as OMR or OCR. No typing is done.

10 a D b C c D d C e A f B

11 Redundancy / inconsistency / poor reliability or integrity of data.

12 Relational database / relationships / table / data redundancy / data integrity

13 A term which describes how easily data can be transferred between one system and another.

14 a It makes the file smaller.
b A data compression utility.
c First decompress the file, then open it.
d Files are made smaller and use up less storage space.

15 C

16 CSV files are simple text files. Data in CSV form can be read and understood by word processors, databases and spreadsheets.

Chapter C2(c) Revision questions

LANs and WANs

1 a Local Area Network
b Wide Area Network
c World Wide Web
d Internet Service Provider
e HyperText Mark-up Language
f Uniform Resource Locator
g Integrated Services Digital Network
h Public Switched Telephone Network
i Asymmetric Digital Subscriber Line
j Personal Computer

2 a A network of computers linked together across a small geographic area.
b Students should draw their own diagram.
c A single connection point for a group of computers. The switch allows up to 22 computers to be connected to it directly using network cables.

3 a An agreed standard for sending or receiving data on a computer network.
b A network of computers linked together across a large geographic area.
c E.g. cables, satellite communication links.
d To link other branches together / to communication like e-mail

4 a ADSL / PSTN / ISDN
b ADSL – can perform a variety of activities such as video conferencing. Broadband means quicker communication.

5 a Peripherals like printers and scanners can be shared between a number of computers / software stored on the file server can be shared by all the computers on the network / users can share files and work on joint projects using shared resources on the network / users have flexible access, they can log on at any computer and access their files / communication between computers and users can be done easily using e-mail or conferencing.
b Expensive to implement / specialist technical knowledge required to manage it.

6 a The World Wide Web
b Apart from computer, telecommunications line, modem
c ISP software, browser software
d A variety of bandwidth options / an e-mail service with virus protection / web hosting service which allows users to upload their own web pages / online and telephone assistance / junk mail blocker / pop-up advert blocker / website filtering which will filter out unsuitable content
e On a network, the rate at which data can be transmitted along the communications line in a given period of time.
f Larger bandwidth means a quicker download time.
g E.g. Yahoo!, Google.
h Filtering options
i E.g. address bar / bookmarks / navigation bar

7

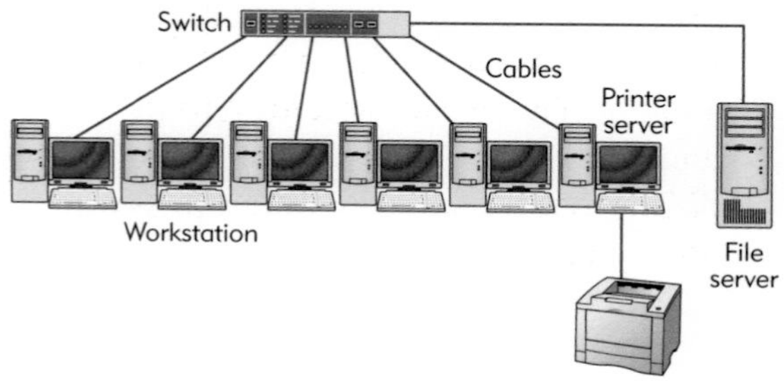

8 a 56kbps
b 128kbps
c up to 8MBps
d >=1Gb

9 http:// – The protocol used to exchange information (in this case HyperText Mark-up Language).

www.google.co.uk – The domain name which includes the name of the host server (in this case Google).

uk – The country level domain name (in this case the United Kingdom).

Network security

10 a Each user sets their own password known only to them. The system requires a correct username and password match before access is provided.
b Giving different people different access rights. For example a teacher has more access rights than a pupil.
c Data is encoded and can only be decoded using the correct 'key'.

11 a A second copy of a file kept for security reasons.
b Daily on magnetic tape
c Weekly on CD-R.

Internet communication systems

12 Digital camera: can be expensive to buy / photos can be downloaded to a PC and edited or manipulated using a graphics package / not all photos need to be printed – the user can delete unwanted photos from memory / no expensive developing costs – the digital photos can be printed on a home printer / no waiting to see photos – they can be viewed on the LCD screen immediately / photo quality can vary according to the output device producing them / photos are in JPEG format and can be e-mailed or placed in other documents.

Conventional camera: cheaper to buy / hardcopy of photos only is produced / all photos in the film have to be printed – wasteful and expensive if the photos are not of good quality / the exposed film has to be developed and printed by a specialist – this is an expensive process / the photographer has to wait until photos are developed before viewing them / photos are of a very high quality / hardcopy of the photos have to be scanned if they are to be used in digital documents.

13 e-mail / texting / voice telephone calls

14 The salesperson can remain in touch with the office / can collect e-mails / can use information services provided on the Internet.

15 Video conferencing technology. The following equipment is needed: a video camera or webcam to transmit pictures; microphone and sound system to transmit and receive sound; a screen to view other participants; a high bandwidth telecommunications line; videoconferencing software.

Chapter C2(d) Revision questions

1

Acronym/ abbreviation	Explanation
EFT	Electronic Funds Transfer
POS	Point of Sale
EPOS	Electronic Point of Sale
EFTPOS	Electronic Funds Transfer Point of Sale
ATM	Automatic Teller (Telling) Machine
PIN	Personal Identification Number
ADC	Analogue to digital converter

2

Input devices in an EFTPOS	Output devices at an EFTPOS	Processing devices at an EFTPOS
Barcode reader Keypad	Printer Screen	CPU for processing barcode entries

3
1. The barcode scanner reads the barcode on the product.
2. The barcode is sent by the EFTPOS terminal to the branch's computer (containing the stock database).
3. The computer uses the barcode to search the stock file looking for a matching product.
4. When the product is found, the product price and product description are sent back to the EFTPOS terminal.
5. The branch's computer updates the stock level for the product to show that one (or more) has been sold.

4 D A C B

5 Advantages to the customer: customers get their credit card slips automatically printed at the checkout / customers using debit cards can also obtain cash at the checkout / the money involved in the transaction is debited from customer account immediately so the balance displayed in the account is always up to date / some customers feel more secure if they don't have to carry large amounts of cash in their wallet/purse / credit/debit card can be used in any country – local currency is not needed for purchases.
Advantages to the vendor: payment to the shop's bank account is guaranteed as long as the transactions are properly authorised / less administration/paperwork so less staff required / reduced concerns with forged monies / the shop collects less cash so there is less chance of theft / if the money is deposited immediately in the shop's bank account they may receive more interest.

6 a withdrawing cash (with or without a receipt) / ordering a bank statement / ordering new chequebook / getting your current account balance / printing a mini-statement (usually the most recent transactions) / informing customers of new banking services / top up mobile phone credit / change PIN.

b Entry of PIN number entered a maximum of three times.

c There is no need for customers to carry large amounts of cash, as ATMs are widely available, hence less theft / customers have access, 24 hours a day and 7 days a week to their accounts / saves money because banks need fewer employees behind counters as fewer customers use the bank / people can use ATMs that don't belong to their bank, which provides access from all over the world.

d It is impossible for a customer to withdraw cash from their account unless they have sufficient funds / using a PIN number is more secure than using a signature on a cheque to obtain cash.

7 a Magnetic stripe: designed to store only a small amount of data; data on the magnetic stripe can be easily corrupted if exposed to magnetic field
Microchip: can store more data than a typical magnetic stripe; almost completely unaffected by magnetic field.

b Highly flexible technology which means they can be used in many applications. More secure than magnetic stripe alone.

c mobile phones (SIM card) /satellite TV receivers (e.g. SKY TV cards) / prepaid phone cards / retail loyalty schemes / personal identification / access to buildings

8 a D b C

9 a Stores information which does not change between bills, such as customer account number, customer name, address details etc.

b Is a temporary file. It contains the customer account number and the current meter reading.
c This information will be used to update the master file.
d Error report and bills.

10 Helmets / gloves / headphones / goggles

11 a Training / gaming / building design
b Surgeons can plan and practise (simulate) a particular operation on the 'virtual patient' before actually carrying it out on a real patient / they can predict the outcome of the operation using this technique.

12 a A b A c D

13 Greenhouse control / traffic control / domestic control systems

14 Shopping / reservations / e-commerce / banking

15 Internet is now readily available on a home PC including cheaper local call access anywhere in the world / growing volumes of information on a wide variety of topics such as electronic catalogues / valuable learning resource for customers because Internet skills may be required for their jobs / a range of product reviews can be obtained before deciding to make a purchase / goods are normally cheaper than buying on the high street / customers normally get free delivery when they purchase over a certain quantity or value / you can buy goods from anywhere in the world which means you are not restricted to shopping in your own town or city / search engines can assist the user to precisely locate what they need / multimedia format of the Internet makes it attractive and easier for customers to use / other services such as e-mail can be used by customers to request more information / customers can shop 24 hours a day, seven days a week.

16 Worldwide client access so a business can have a larger customer base, both locally and globally / the business can communicate with customers immediately such as supplying product information and specifications (including graphics) through online electronic catalogues / the use of the Internet allows a business to advertise new products and current promotions cheaply compared with using national newspapers / new clients can be found without the need for employing salespeople / update product information frequently and immediately / quick and cheap method of doing market research on customer views / assess the impact of Internet by using a count of those who visit the site / Fewer staff and overheads because no premises are required to sell stock.

Chapter 3

Revision questions

Multiple choice questions

1 C 2 C 3 A 4 D 5 D 6 D
7 B 8 B 9 A 10 C

True or false?

1 T 2 F 3 F 4 T 5 T 6 T
7 T 8 T 9 T 10 T

Match a word to a statement

1 C 2 E 3 F 4 G 5 A 6 D
7 H 8 B

Index

3.5 inch floppy disks 35–6

acronyms and abbreviations 8, 27, 44, 58, 74, 96–7, 113–14
ADC (Analogue to Digital Converter) 85
ADSL (Asymmetric Digital Subscriber Line) 62
aircraft simulators 83–4
applications of ICT
  Automatic Teller Machines (ATMs) 77–9
  billing applications 80–2
  control systems 85–8
  electronic monetary processing 75–7
  magnetic stripe and smart cards 79–80
  online services 88–9
  virtual reality 82–4
ASCII (American Standard Code for Information Interchange) files 52
ATMs (Automatic Teller Machines) 77–9

back pain, minimising risk of 101
backups 61
bandwidth 62–3
banking 77–9, 88
barcodes/barcode readers 76
batch processing systems 80–2
BCC (Blind Carbon Copy) 12
billing applications 80–2
bits (Binary digITs) 34
browser software 9, 65
building designs, virtual reality used in 83
bulletin boards 69
bus networks 60
businesses, effects of online services 88–9
bytes 34

cable connection 63
cache memory 30
CAL (Computer-Assisted Learning) 98
cameras 31–2, 70–1
car park management, control systems 87
cash machines 77–9
CC (carbon copy) 12
CD-R (Compact Disk-Recordable) 36
CD-ROM (Compact Disk–Read-Only Memory) 36
CD-RW (Compact Disk – Rewriteable) 36
CDs (compact disks) 36
central processing unit (CPU) 28
characters 34
check digits 47
Chip and Pin systems 77
communication technologies in education 99
communications protocols 63
compact disks (CDs) 36
components of ICT system 28
  CPU (central processing unit) 28
  input devices 30–2
  output devices 32–4
  storage devices 34–7
compression of data 52–3
compression, file 97, 104
Computer Misuse Act (1990) 106
computer models and simulation 82–3
conferencing 69
connection types 62–3
control systems 85–8
Copyright Designs and Patents Act (1988) 106–7
CPU (central processing unit) 28
CRT (cathode ray tube) monitors 32
CSV (Comma Separated Variable) files 51

data 44–5
  capture 47–8
  checking 46–7
  collecting for processing 45
  compression 52–3
  logging 85, 86, 87
  portability 51–2
  security of 60–1
  structure 48–9
  types 46
data logging 85, 86, 87
Data Protection Act (1998) 107–8
database software 18–19
databases
  flat files 48–9
  relational 49–51
  software 18–19
definitions 8–9, 97
desktop publishing (DTP) software 15–16
digital cameras 31–2, 70–1
digital signatures 97, 106
digital TV (DTV) 70, 103
digital versatile disks (DVDs) 36–7
domain names 65
domestic control systems 87–8
dot matrix printers 32
dpi (dots per inch) 32, 33
DTP software 15–16
DTV (digital TV) 70, 103
DVDs (Digital Versatile Disks) 36–7

e-commerce 88, 97, 106
e-mail software 12–13, 67–8
education, impact of ICT on 98–9
EFT (Electronic Funds Transfer) 75, 77
EFTPOS (Electronic Funds Transfer Point of Sale) 75–6

electricity bill, stages in producing 81–2
electronic monetary processing 75–7
ELF (Extremely Low Frequency) radiation 103
employment, impact of ICT on 99–100
encryption 60, 106
EPOS (Electronic Point of Sale) 75
external hard disks 35
eyestrain, minimising 102

facsimile (fax) machines 68–9
FAST (The Federation Against Software Theft) 107
feedback in control systems 85–8
fibre optic cable 63
fields, database 48, 50, 51
file servers 59
files
  compression of 97, 104
  flat files 48–9
  master and transaction files 81
  portable file types 51–2
firewalls 60, 97
flash storage devices 37
flat files 48–9
forms for data collection 45

games industry, impact of ICT 104
games, virtual reality in 84
GB (gigabyte) 34
GIF (Graphic Interchange Format) files 52
gigabyte (GB) 34
graphics software 17–18
greenhouse control systems 86
GUI (Graphical User Interface) 29

hard disks 34–5
health and safety issues 101–3
home-based employment 100
home heating systems, temperature control 85
home and leisure, impact of ICT on 103–6
HTML (HyperText Markup Language) 65
HTTP (HyperText Transfer Protocol) 65

ICC (integrated chip card) 80
image systems 70–1
information 44–5
ink-jet printers 33
input devices 30–2
instant messaging 69
integrity of data 49
Internet
  connecting to 63–4
  and education 98
  online services 88–9
  WAP phones 70
intranets 66–7
ISDN (Integrated Services Digital Network) 62
ISPs (Internet Service Providers) 64

jobs, effects of ICT on 99–100
joysticks 31
JPEG (Joint Photographic Experts Group) files 51

key fields 50, 51
keyboards 30
kilobyte (KB) 34

LANs (Local Area Networks) 58–9
  components of 59–60
  security of 60–1
laser printers 33
laws and ICT 106–8
LCD (Liquid Crystal Display) 31, 33
leisure pursuits, impact of ICT on 103–6

macros 9, 20
magnetic storage devices 34–6
magnetic stripes 79
magnetic tape streamers 35
MB (megabyte) 34
medicine, virtual reality in 84
megabyte (MB) 34
memory, types of computer 29–30
mice 30–1
microphones 31
MIDI (Musical Instrument Digital Interface) files 52
mobile phones 69–70
modelling see spreadsheet software
modem (MOdulator-DEModulator) 64
monitors 33–4
MP3 files 52, 97, 104
MPEG (Moving Picture Experts Group) files 51
music industry, impact of ICT 103–4

networks
  connection types 62–3
  differences between LANs and WANs 62
  file server 59
  hardware 59–60
  Local Area Networks (LANs) 58–61
  network topology 60
  software 60
  Wide Area Networks (WANs) 61

OCR (Optical Character Recognition) 32, 48
OMR (Optical Mark Recognition) 47
online services 88–9
operating systems 28–9
optical storage devices 36–7
output devices 32–4

PDAs (Portable Digital Assistants) 70
personal data 108
phones 69–70
PICT files 51
PIN (Personal Identification Number) 77, 78, 79
piracy 106
pixels 34
plotters 33
portability of data 50–1
POS (Point of Sale) 75
ppm (pages per minute) 33
presentation software 16–17
primary key 9
printer resolution 33
printers 32–3
processors, computer hardware 28
protocols, communication 63
PSTN (Public Switched Telephone Network) 62

radiation exposure 102
RAM (Random Access Memory) 29–30
real-time processing 85
records 48
redundancy 49
relational databases 9, 18–19, 49–51

reservations, online 88
resolution
  printers 33
  screen 34
ring networks 60
ROM (Read Only Memory) 30
routers 61
RSI (Repetitive Strain Injury) 101
RTF (Rich Text Format) files 51

safety issues 101–3
satellite connection 63
scanners 32
screen resolution 34
search engines 9–10
security
  of a network 60–1
  online shopping 105–6
sensors, control systems 85–8
SET (Secure Electronic Transaction) 106
shopping, impact of ICT 105–6
simulations 82–4
smart cards 80
SMS (Short Message Service) 69
software piracy 106
speakers 34
speed control systems 87
spreadsheet software 19–20
star networks 59, 60
storage devices 34–7
SVGA (Super Video Graphics Array) 34

tables 9, 11, 14, 15, 18–19, 49–50
TCP/IP (Transmission Control Protocol / Internet Protocol) 63
television 70, 103
teleworking 100
temperature control 85, 86
templates 8, 11, 13, 14, 15
text messages 69
TFT (Thin Film Transistor) monitors 33–4
TIFF (Tagged Image Format) files 52
touch screens 32
tracker pads 31
traffic control systems 86–7
traffic lights 86
TXT (Text File) format 52

URLs (Uniform Resource Locators) 65
USB Flash drives 37
user interface 29

validation of data 46–7
VDUs (Visual Display Units) 33
verification of data 46
video conferencing 69
video industry, impact of ICT 104–5
virtual reality systems 82–4
virus protection 61
VLEs (Virtual Learning Environments) 99
volatile and non-volatile memory 29–30

WANs (Wide Area Networks) 61
WAP (Wireless Application Protocol) 63
WAP phones 70
washing machine, control systems 87–8
web browser software 9, 65
web creation software 11–12
WIMP (Windows, Icons, Menus, Pointers) 29
wizards 8, 14, 16
word-processing software 13–14
workplace safety 103
WORM (Write-Once Read-Many) 36
WWW (World Wide Web) 66

zip disks 35